# SHIP AGENCY

## A Guide to Tramp Ship Agency Practice

### Third Edition

D1609850

# Marygrace Collins
# Kenneth Schiels
# Peter Skoufalos

WITHERBY **Seamanship**
INTERNATIONAL

**Witherby Seamanship International**
A Division of Witherby Publishing Group Ltd

4 Dunlop Square, Livingston, Edinburgh, EH54 8SB, Scotland, UK
Tel No: +44(0)1506 463 227 - Fax No: +44(0)1506 468 999
Email: info@emailws.com - Web: www.witherbyseamanship.com

First edition published 1987
Second edition published 1995
Third edition published 2013
Reprinted 2013

ISBN: 978-1-85609-585-3
eBook ISBN: 978-1-85609-587-7


© Witherby Publishing Group Ltd, 2013

**British Library Cataloguing in Publication Data**
A catalogue record for this book is available from the British Library.

Printed and bound in Great Britain by Bell & Bain Ltd, Glasgow

Published by

**Witherby Publishing Group Ltd**
4 Dunlop Square, Livingston,
Edinburgh, EH54 8SB,
Scotland, UK

Tel No: +44(0)1506 463 227
Fax No: +44(0)1506 468 999

Email: info@emailws.com
Web: www.witherbys.com

# Dedication

We wish to thank our spouses, Kevin, Jean and Ellen, and our children, for supporting our maritime careers when all too often our attention had to be given to the needs of the ships.

Marygrace Collins

Kenneth Schiels

Peter Skoufalos

# Preface to the Third Edition

Except for the pilot, the first and last person to board or depart during every ship's port call is the ship's agent. In tramp shipping, both in dry bulk and tanker, the selection of the port agent at the load and discharge port is part of charter party negotiations.

The shipping industry is a vast and complicated business. Due to the many types of ships, and the charter parties by which they are contracted, the training of boarding agents or water clerks can be a long and complex process. Hopefully this book will make the process easier. It will also provide ship owners and charterers with an understanding of the function of the ship agent.

This book will introduce a basic knowledge of the industry and encourage people entering shipping to further their education. The first few chapters cover basic marine transportation. The middle chapters provide insight into the legal relationships between the agent, the principal and third parties. The final chapters are gleaned from the authors' experiences of working from the bottom up.

Each of the three authors has worked in shipping for over thirty years. We have contributed to this book our background in port agency operations, ship brokerage and operations and maritime law.

Marygrace, Peter and Ken hope we have tweaked your curiosity about the world of ship agency.

# The Authors' Biographic Backgrounds

The origin of the book was a graduate school thesis at the State University of New York Maritime College, written by Kenneth Schiels in 1984. The manuscript became the first edition of *Tramp Ship Agency Practice,* published by Lloyd's of London Press in 1987. The second edition was published by Fairplay in 1994 as *Ship Agency: A Guide to Tramp Ship Agency.* We are pleased to give to the reader the third edition, combining the first two edition titles of *Ship Agency – A Guide to Tramp Ship Agency Practice.*

The third edition has three co-authors. Marygrace Collins is a partner in Bulkore Chartering, Inc, a dry bulk cargo ship broker located in New York. Bulkore is a full service dry cargo ship broking shop. However, as the name implies, their forte lies heavily on the carriage of iron ore from mines to mills all over the globe.

Marygrace was the first woman to serve as President of the Association of Ship Brokers and Agents (USA) Inc, in 2004 and 2005. She remains active in ASBA, and is a moderator for the Association's Home Study Course, "The Basic Principles of Chartering". She also serves on the Executive Committee of FONASBA – The Federation of National Associations of Ship Brokers and Agents, headquartered in London, and was elected President of FONASBA in October 2012. Marygrace is also a member of Women's International Shipping & Trading Association (WISTA) and the Connecticut Maritime Association. She has a Bachelor of Science degree from Georgetown University.

Peter Skoufalos concentrates in the areas of commercial and maritime law as a partner in the New York-based firm of Brown, Gavalas & Fromm. In his practice he advises key players in the maritime transportation sector, including ship agents and other intermediaries. Peter is a graduate of New York University and the Boston University School of Law. Peter has authored several articles on maritime law and is currently Vice-Chairman of the US Maritime Law Association Sub Committee on Arbitration and Mediation. Peter has been involved with this book from its beginning in 1984 and has helped simplify some of the complex legal issues that agents occasionally confront.

Kenneth Schiels obtained a Bachelor of Science degree at Saint Francis University in Pennsylvania and his Masters of Science degree at the State University of New York Maritime College. His career has been in ships agency as a boarding agent, port manager, and an executive for a national ship agency in the United States. He is the owner of a marketing firm providing sales representation for international shipping agency firms into the North American shipping industry. Ken is on the Education Committee and the Agency Affairs Committee for ASBA, the Association of Ship Brokers and Agents (USA) Inc.

# Acknowledgements

The authors wish to thank the following for their important contributions towards the source material of this book.

C.F.H. Cufley, *Ocean Freight and Chartering*, London: Granada Publishing, 1970.

Chapter 1, 2, 3, 4, 5.

Lane C. Kendall, *The Business of Shipping*, 4th rev. ed., Centreville:

Cornell Maritime Press, 1983.

Chapter 1, 2, 3, 4.

W. Edward Sell, *Sell on Agency*, New York: The Foundation Press Inc, 1975.

Chapter 1, 6, 8, 9.

William Sembler, Professor of Advanced Chartering Problems I, State University of New York, Maritime College, New York, Lectures 1982.

Chapter 3.

# Contents

Dedication                                                                iii
Preface to the Third Edition                                               v
The Authors' Biographic Backgrounds                                      vii
Acknowledgements                                                          ix

Chapter 1    Tramp Ship Agency and the International Shipping Industry      1
1.1    Definition of 'Agency'                                              1
1.2    The Shipping Industry as a Service                                  1
1.3    The Liner Business of Shipping                                      2
1.4    The Tramp Ship Owner                                               4

Chapter 2    Tramp Shipping                                                7
2.1    Tramp Ship Owners and Operators                                     7
2.2    Dry Bulk Carriers                                                   8
2.3    Liquid Bulk Carriers                                                9
2.4    Tramp Vessel Operations and Management                             9
2.5    The Commercial Operating of Ships                                  11
2.6    Types of Employment for Tramp Vessels                              11
2.7    The Freight Market                                                 13

Chapter 3    Shipbroking                                                  15
3.1    Types of Shipbrokers                                               16
3.2    The Freight Market                                                 17

Chapter 4    Tramp Ship Agency Practice                                   19
4.1    Port Agency Companies                                              19
4.2    Tramp Agency Operation                                             19
4.3    Pre-arrival                                                        20
4.4    The Port Call                                                      21
4.5    After Sailing Service                                              23
4.6    Functions of Agency Staff Members                                  24

Chapter 5    Defining Tramp Agency and the Scope of Services Provided      27
5.1    General Agent                                                      27
5.2    Special Agent                                                      29
5.3    The Right to Select the Port Agent                                 30
5.4    Charterer's Nominated Agents                                       30
5.5    Hub Agent                                                          32
5.6    Other Outsource Agency Services                                    34

**Chapter 6     The Law of Agency**                                                          **35**

6.1     The Relationship of Agency                                               35
6.2     The Creation of Agency                                                      36
6.3     Agency by Necessity                                                          36
6.4     Ratification by Principals                                                   37
6.5     Termination of the Agency Relationship                             38

**Chapter 7     The Ship's Agent, Principals and Third Parties**                            **41**

7.1     The Disclosed Principal                                                     41
7.2     The Partly-Disclosed Principal                                          42
7.3     The Undisclosed Principal                                                 42
7.4     Third Party Rights Against Agent and Principal in the United Kingdom     43
7.5     Third Party Rights Against Agent and Principal in the United States      43
7.6     The Weakness of the 'As Agent' Signature                         44
7.7     Creation of a Maritime Lien in the United States                 45
7.8     Ship Agent's Right to a Lien                                              46

**Chapter 8     Duties and Liabilities of the Agent to the Principal**                       **49**

8.1     Duty to Act within the Scope of Authority                         49
8.2     The Agent's Duty of Confidentiality and Loyalty               50
8.3     Duty and Liability to Contract on the Principal's Behalf     51
8.4     The Importance of Contract Signature                             52
8.5     The Duty to Account for Funds Advanced by the Principal     52
8.6     The Duty to Exercise Care, Skill and Diligence                 52
8.7     Duty of the Agent to Perform all Duties Personally            53
8.8     Duty to Keep the Principal Informed                               53
8.9     Notification of Principal Through the Agent                      54

**Chapter 9     Principal's Duties and Liability to the Agent**                              **57**

9.1     The Principal's Duty to Provide an Opportunity for Work     57
9.2     The Principal's Duty of Good Conduct                            58
9.3     The Principal's Duty to Pay Compensation                      58
9.4     Remedies of an Agent                                                     59

**Chapter 10    Indemnity Insurance for Agents**                                            **61**

10.1    Protection Coverage for Ship Agents                             61
10.2    When Agents are most Vulnerable to Claims                  63

**Chapter 11    Duties under a Time Charter or as a Voyage Charterer's
                        Nominated Agent**                                                            **65**

11.1    Voyage Charterer's Nominated Agent                            65
11.2    Ship Agent's Duty Under Time Charter                          68
11.3    Disbursements Under Time Charter                              71
11.4    Attendance of Delivery and Redelivery                          72

Chapter 12   How to Select a Tramp Ship Agent                                    75

12.1   The Agent is a Reflection of the Party who Nominates or Appoints          75
12.2   Financial Strength                                                         76
12.3   The Reporting of Voyage Accounting                                         76
12.4   Communication and Cargo Documentation                                     77
12.5   Company and Agency Staff Experience                                        78
12.6   Worldwide Ship Agency Networks                                            78

Chapter 13   Maintenance of the Agent/Principal Relationship                    81

13.1   The Personal Relationship and Corporate Relationship                      81
13.2   The Trade Relationship                                                     83

Chapter 14   Charterer's Liability for Actions of a Nominated Agent              85

14.1   The Charter Party Agency Clause                                           85
14.2   The Incentive for a Voyage Charterer to Nominate the Port Agent           86
14.3   The Charterer must Make a Reasonable Appointment                          86
14.4   Liability for the Insolvency of the Agent                                 88
14.5   Charterer's Liability Through the Implied Agency Doctrine                  88
14.6   Charterer's Liability in Cases Where the Nominated Agent is Acting
       for a Limited Purpose                                                     89
14.7   The Ship Owner's Ratification of the Charterer's Agency Nomination        89

Chapter 15   Managing a Tramp Ship Agency                                       91

15.1   Tramp Agency Fees                                                         91
15.2   Service Fees                                                              92
15.3   Accounting                                                                95
15.4   Communications                                                            96
15.5   Staffing                                                                  99

Chapter 16   Tramp Ship Agency Marketing                                        101

16.1   Selling to an Owner                                                       104
16.2   Selling to a Charterer                                                    105
16.3   Planning a Sales Call                                                     106

Chapter 17   The Tramp Ship Agency Career                                       109

Chapter 18   Authors' Thoughts                                                  113

Bibliography                                                                     115
Abbreviations                                                                    117
Basics of Ship Charters                                                          123
Frequently used Shipping Terms                                                   127
Index                                                                            131

# Chapter 1
## Tramp Ship Agency and the International Shipping Industry

---

## 1.1     Definition of 'Agency'

A fiduciary relationship exists between the agent and his principal. A good definition of 'agency' is:

> "Agency is the name given to the legal relationship which arises when two parties enter into an agreement, whereby one of the parties, called the agent, agrees to represent or act for the other called the principal, subject to the principal's right to control the agent's conduct concerning the matters entrusted to him".

W Edward Sell, Dean, University of Pittsburgh School of Law.

This book is about the relationship between the ship owner or charterer, as principal, and the port agent, as agent, to whom the ship owner or charterer entrusts his vessel's operations, management and care. The agent's purpose is to protect the principal's interest at a specific port, where the agent is domiciled, in accordance with the instructions and authority granted by the ship owner.

> The fiduciary relationship will be studied in depth in Chapter 8. To understand the agency relationship between the ship owner and agent, the economic environment of international trade and the function of the ship owner within it must be described.

## 1.2     The Shipping Industry as a Service

The growth of civilization and commerce, combined with movements of empire and colonization, has created a global shipping industry. Changes in bases of manufacturing power, differing requirements for raw materials and new bases of economic power have meant that the marketing and transportation of goods have grown in complexity and volume, creating today's international freight market.

The shipping community serves industry by building and operating a wide variety of ships, such as tanker vessels, bulk carriers, container ships, LPG and LNG carriers, heavy lift ships, refrigerator ships, cruise ships and various other specialized vessels, all designed to serve the economic community and the need to bring the world's goods to markets when and where demanded.

Industrial nations will have raw materials delivered in bulk by tramp vessels. Finished products are transported from the industrial nations into the world market via liner vessels serving ports throughout the world at regular intervals. Because of the scope of international trade, the shipping industry has developed into two main types, liner shipping and tramp shipping.

Tramp vessels are designed to carry large volumes of homogeneous raw materials and foodstuffs from supplier nations to user nations. These will be converted into finished goods of high value requiring distribution on vessels with scheduled departures from producing centers to consumer nations.

It is this fundamental difference between liner and tramp shipping that this book separates. Each branch of shipping requires agents at ports throughout the world, but the agency services rendered will differ, depending on the type of shipping service that the agent's principals are engaged in.

# 1.3    The Liner Business of Shipping

A liner service is a common carrier, rather than a contract carrier. Liner companies usually own and operate a number of ships that serve one or more established trade routes between geographical areas. Because of the liner companies' repetitive arrival and departure dates, which are advertised among specific ports between two geographic areas, businesses that trade in commodities of a few tons up to hundreds of tons are able to market and distribute their goods on a regular delivery basis to overseas consumers.

The fact that industry can ship high-value goods between overseas nations without having to hire an entire vessel for one voyage has enabled international trade to flourish and allow producer nations to expand their markets beyond their nation's borders. Examples include:

- Cars from Japan
- advanced computer technology from the USA
- fruit from South America.

Liner cargoes generally consist of several hundred different lots and types of commodities, all loaded into one vessel. Liner trade cargo is generally of higher value than the bulk homogeneous commodities carried on tramp vessels. As less than ship-load lots are carried on liner vessels, they charge higher rates. Due to the vast spectrum of cargoes carried by the liner, a tariff is used to quote freight rates based on the commodity, its volume and its destination within the liner service.

Terms of carriage are based on a contract called the 'standard liner bill of lading', which is issued by the liner company. All terms of carriage are stated on the bill of lading (B/L) and are rarely negotiable. Contract terms of the B/L apply to all shippers, regardless of commodity.

Trade routes are often competitive between two or more liner companies. The number of shippers and the volume of traffic generated by each port within the geographical range of ports determine the frequency of service and the rates charged by the liner companies. Their ability to provide reliable arrival and departure dates in accordance with their advertisements, as well as personalized service to shippers, determines the line's competitiveness with the other lines trading in the same route. To meet the shippers' demands in a specific route, liner companies built their vessels in accordance with the ports and cargo of the shipper. Over the years, fully containerized vessels, have taken over the route from general cargo ships. In some parts of the world, where ports and terminals are not always as modern as those of the major Western industrial nations, general cargo vessels with onboard lifting gear are employed, and these will have a capability for container carriage.

Due to the regularity of port calls and the variability of cargo types and shippers, the liner operation requires a large and complex organization. The home office may consist of a marketing department, vessel husbandry, engineering department, documentation department, insurance and claims, freight department, terminal operations, fleet management, personnel department, sales staff, container control, IT Department and booking clerks. Because of the liner company's large organization and staff requirements, it is not economically feasible to have company offices in every port it serves. It is also common for liner companies to be domiciled in countries other than those that they service. Where it does not have its own office, the liner company employs a general agent, who may be capable of covering a range of ports within the geographical range served by the line. The general agent's responsibilities are outlined in the 'standard liner agency contract', which details the agent's responsibility and authority to act on behalf of the liner company. The agents will have an office staff organized in a similar manner to the liner company. The marketing department of the agent will consist of salespeople who will be in regular sales contact with shippers and freight forwarders who have traffic on the trade route of the line.

The departments that a general agent will need to properly represent a liner company are sales, traffic, documentation, freight cashier, booking, manifesting, container control and an agency department that attends to the vessel's husbandry matters similar to a tramp vessel. Remuneration for the general agent's service is a percentage commission based on the freight booked on the liner vessel's call at the port. The liner company may also agree to pay the general agent additional service fees such as container control, ship husbandry, trucking, and also reimburse the agent for certain expenses that the agent will incur servicing the line.

# 1.4    The Tramp Ship Owner

The tramp ship owner or operator is a contract carrier and the ships are chartered to carry anything anywhere. The tramp vessel does not have advertised sailings between ports. Tramp vessel cargoes are homogeneous bulk commodities usually carried between two ports for one shipper, under one contract for which terms and conditions are negotiated.

For early ship owners, the tramp vessels represented all their wealth. Every penny spent for maintenance was a penny less profit for the owner, so maintenance was usually the last thing they spent money on. As a result, the ships ended up looking as bad as the women that frequented dockside bars. Today, the name 'tramp' only categorizes a vessel type and method of trading in the shipping market. Tramp ship owners invest sufficient money into vessel maintenance programs to comply with flag and Classification requirements, which are strictly enforced. They market themselves to charterers as having a vessel capable of carrying their cargo in a safe and efficient manner. Delays in port to conduct repairs, and resulting loss of on the charter market, has become the primary reason for scheduled maintenance programs on tramp vessels.

The tramp vessel is built as a single deck vessel, similar to a floating box. Some tramp vessels are built with a tween deck, which is a second interior deck that enables the vessel to carry general cargo,

Freight rates are not published as a tariff. Supply and demand controls the tramp freight market. An 'owner's market' is where the demand for vessels to carry cargo from an area exceeds the supply, which allows the owner to demand a higher rate for his vessel. A 'charterer's market' is where there are many vessels positioned in an area, with few cargoes looking for vessels. Because tramp vessels wander the oceans in search of cargoes, they are built with the flexibility to carry commodities that are shipped in bulk, such as coal, ores, bauxite, sugar, salt, cement, scrap metal, grain and semi-finished products. These commodities move between supplier and user nations, so the ship owners will try to arrange a return cargo to be loaded at or near the discharge port. This type of trading maximizes the use of the vessel and its revenue earning ability. A tramp vessel travelling in ballast, without cargo, is losing money. The same applies when the vessel is awaiting her next orders of employment.

Tramp vessel operation does not require a large staff to run the company. A small number of people functioning effectively can handle the crewing, bunker supply orders, claims, accounting, husbandry, insurance, chartering, and other matters, avoiding the high costs of overheads that are incurred by the liner operator.

Due to the vast number of tramp vessels and the bulk commodities they carry, tramp owners obtain cargo commitments and charterers seek vessels through the charter market. This is not a physical place, but is an international network of shipbrokers representing ship owners and charterers. Due to the large population of both owners and charterers, they usually contact each other through their appointed brokers.

The main shipbroking centers are London, New York, and Singapore. Advances in communications have resulted in the creation of many more regional shipbroking centers throughout the world.

Ship owners seeking employment for their vessels advise their brokers accordingly. The broker distributes the vessel's name, vessel description and present position to shipbrokers representing charterers seeking vessels. When a charterer's broker becomes aware of a vessel of specific dimensions and dates available, he contacts the owner's broker describing the cargo, the quantity, the dates and place for loading, as well as the freight rate per ton the charterer is willing to offer the owner for this business. In turn, the owner's broker advises the ship owner of the cargo the charterer is willing to offer. Negotiations commence between owner and charterer through the intermediary brokers.

Like the liner ship operator, the tramp ship owner obviously cannot have a branch office in every port throughout the world. Due to the uncertainty of the next employment, the tramp owner will appoint a ship agent at the load and discharge port to represent and protect the interests of himself and his vessel, in accordance with the terms and conditions of the contract of carriage, i.e. the charter party, and to deal with the local port authorities and government regulations that apply to the owner's vessel.

> **It is to this agent, who is employed by the tramp ship owner, that this book is largely directed. Because of the uncertainty of visiting any one port, a general agency agreement is not suitable for a tramp owner. Therefore, his relationship with the port agent servicing a tramp vessel occurs without predetermined regularity, creating different legal implications and liability than with the general agent.**

The tramp ship owner's agent will perform whatever functions are required to operate, manage and assist the Master of the vessel to comply with local government regulations and the charter party, all as if the ship owner were present in the port. All the agent's actions on behalf of the owner are undertaken only upon instructions and authorization granted by the ship owner and/or the vessel's Master. The tramp ship agent receives remuneration based either on the tariff in effect in that port, or as negotiated between the owner and the agent. A detailed study of the agent and owner as principal relationship will develop in later chapters.

# Chapter 2
## Tramp Shipping

To understand tramp ship agency, it is necessary to have an understanding of the tramp ship operator and vessel operation.

Tramp shipping can be generalized as having no advertised sailings; it involves a flexible ship designed to carry one or more types of homogeneous bulk commodities or general cargo. The vessels are contract carriers carrying goods under one contract, generally between two ports. Remuneration is determined by the forces of supply and demand of vessels and cargoes available at a particular place and time.

Historically, tramp shipping can be traced to the industrial revolution, when manufacturing first began to use steam engines. Raw materials were required for processing and energy, sometimes from distant places, so ships were built to carry the various commodities in bulk volumes.

## 2.1 Tramp Ship Owners and Operators

Tramp ship owners range from small firms of one or two vessels, up to larger fleets of as many as hundreds of ships owned and operated by major corporations. Large ship-owning corporations came into being when some industrial companies used their own vessels to carry 'in-house' cargoes, then chartered their vessels into the charter market for a return cargo to pay for costs and avoid a ballast voyage back to the original load port.

International trade for the carriage of ores, grains, fertilizers, coal, sugar and semi-finished goods between producer and consumer nations has created specific groups of bulk tramp vessels, designed and built to serve the shippers' needs for these commodities. Due to the bulk nature of the commonly moved commodities, some ships can be cross traded between commodity types because of the ship's flexibility of design. Tramp shipping may be divided into two principal categories, dry bulk and liquid bulk.

## 2.2    Dry Bulk Carriers

Dry bulk vessels are subdivided into markets based on the commodities carried and the vessel design.

Bulk carriers are characterized by large hatches and deep, wide holds. Self trimming bulk carriers can have holds with sloped bulkheads for the flow of bulk commodity cargoes into the center line of the ship's hold, allowing easy access to shore grabs to get full bucketloads for faster discharge. Bulk carriers may or may not be fitted with cargo handling gear.

Common sizes of bulk carriers:

- Handysize 10,000 to 35,000 DWT

- Handymax 35,000 to 45,000 DWT

- Supramax 45,000 to 62,000 DWT

- Panamax 60,000 to 80,000 DWT

- Post Panamax 80,000 to 110,000 DWT

- Capesize 110,000 to 220,000 DWT

- VLOO 220,000 – 400,000 DWT.

General cargo, or tween deck vessels, normally have cargo gear and a transverse middle deck located between the hold floor and the weather deck. The tween deck runs the length of the vessel. Some vessels are built with decks only in certain holds, for greater flexibility, when used in liner trades with heavy bulk cargoes on the route.

Container ships are vessels designed with holds that have cellular arrangements for the stowage of ISO standard sea containers. Container ships will not usually have cargo gear. These vessels are built to specifications by a liner trader, but they can be spot chartered or time chartered into liner companies, in the same way as tramping, where excess tonnage movements require additional vessels to be brought into the schedule. RoRo vessels (roll on/roll off ships) are designed to carry containers on chassis or vehicles that are driven onto the ship and stowed between decks joined by ramps. RoRo vessels are generally designed for specific trades served by the liner company. Some RoRo vessels operate in the spot trading market for chartering to project cargoes.

Special carriers, such as reefer carriers, are used for the citrus fruit trades. Self unloaders are designed for the bulk gypsum, cement and salt markets. Livestock carriers are used for the transportation of live animals, particularly between Australia and the Middle East.

In general, ships can be built to serve any and all specialized markets, wherever the need and investors are found.

## 2.3    Liquid Bulk Carriers

A liquid bulk carrier is commonly referred to as a tanker. Tankers are best described as a hollow steel shell, subdivided into tanks by longitudinal and transverse bulkheads. A system of pipes, fitted to the tank bottoms and on the weather deck, is joined into a manifold for cargo loading and discharge through the use of cargo pumps.

Tankers are subdivided into categories that are defined by the ship's size and cargo carried, and the category name often provides an indication of geographic draft limits. Handy or small-sized tankers are 6,000 to 35,000 DWT and carry products such as clean petroleum or gas oil, diesel oil, vegetable oils and certain chemicals.

Medium-sized tankers range from 35,000 to 160,000 DWT and are mainly used for crude and heavy fuels. Very large crude carriers (VLCC) range from 160,000 to 400,000 DWT and carry only crude oils, or are used for storage of crude oil where shore tank capacity is full. Ultra large crude carriers (ULCC), the giants of the shipping industry, are over 400,000 DWT. Ships of this size are also used for crude transportation and storage.

Common sizes of tankers:

- Panamax 60,000 to 80,000 DWT

- Aframax 80,000 to 120,000 DWT

- Suezmax 120,000 to 200,000 DWT

- VLCC 200,000 to 315,000 DWT

- ULCC 320,000 to 550,000 DWT.

Gas carriers are vessels built to carry LNG or LPG at very low temperatures and high pressures, which allows the gas to be loaded and carried in liquid form.

Ore/bulk/oil carriers, or OBOs, are vessels designed for both dry bulk and liquid bulk trades. OBOs generally trade in dirty oil cargo or dry bulks such as ores and coal.

## 2.4    Tramp Vessel Operations and Management

A tramp owner of any type requires a smaller staff than that required by a liner operation. Tramp operation functions include, manning, purchasing, engineering/ technical, insurance and claims, chartering and operations.

The purchasing department arranges the purchase of spare parts and forwards them to the vessel's next port. Purchasing also arranges worldwide contracts with chandlers and suppliers. Some purchasing departments arrange for warehousing in strategic locations throughout the world, holding spare parts for a large fleet of ships. Warehousing in a strategic location avoids the loss of time and cost of emergency forwarding of spare parts for engine and cargo gear, which could also delay cargo operations or vessel sailing.

The crewing department arranges for employment of seafarers. Some owners arrange contracts with ship management firms or with crewing companies that recruit in nations where low cost crews can be obtained. Crew costs are the largest overhead in ship operations. An important part of crewing is the training of officers. The high cost of vessel operations requires experienced and reliable personnel. Some owners arrange for the same officers and crews to return to the same vessel time and time again. The scheduling of vacations and sea time is important for the continuity of vessel management. The crewing department also arranges transportation to and from the vessel for crew members and officers coming off leave or repatriating.

Engineering and technical is usually made up of former chief engineers. The superintendent engineer oversees the maintenance programs and any drydocking conducted on the company's vessels. The chief engineers on board a vessel consult with the home office's engineering department for advice on repairs and to order spare parts. In the event of breakdowns of a significant nature, the superintendent engineer from the home office will be sent to coordinate and supervise repairs.

The insurance and claims department is very influential in the control of the trading area, crewing and legal advice. Insurance protects the ship owner financially following physical loss or damage due to collision or loss of a vessel. It also protects the owner against perils named in the insurance policy. The insurance policy covers losses due to total loss, partial loss or particular and general average as well as collisions with other vessels. The underwriters of the insurance policy are not liable to pay for any loss or damage caused by the ship owner's failure to maintain the ship in a seaworthy condition. The insurance underwriters are assured of the vessel's seaworthiness by Classification Societies.

The societies require the vessel to undergo periodic inspections. Provided the vessel is maintained in accordance with the standards of the Classification Society, it will generally remain insured. Members of the International Association of Classification Societies (IACS) are responsible for a classifying the majority of the world fleet.

Protection and indemnity insurance insures the ship owner against losses due to loss of life, personal injury claims, collision with fixed objects and cargo claims. The premium paid by the ship owner to the P&I Club is determined by the managers of the P&I Club, based upon the ship owner's record of losses and claims.

P&I Clubs have worldwide representatives who provide 24-hour service and advice to ship owners whose vessels require assistance or legal action concerning, for example, cargo disputes, oil spills, crew injuries or collisions with berths.

## 2.5    The Commercial Operating of Ships

The tramp chartering operations department arranges cargoes and voyage orders, orders bunkers and appoints agents for the ship owner. Cargoes are sought in the freight market by the chartering department contacting ship owners and or broker/s by providing details of vessel positions and descriptions. The broker/s, in turn, search the freight market for cargoes that correspond with the type of ship operated by the ship owner and that are ready to load in the area where the vessel will come free. The broker acts as the intermediary between the ship owner and the charterer during negotiation of the charter party.

## 2.6    Types of Employment for Tramp Vessels

The ship owner can employ a vessel in three ways:
- Demise (bareboat) charter
- time charter
- voyage charter.

The choice will depend on charter market conditions or the trade in which the ship owner wishes to employ the vessel.

### 2.6.1    Demise (bareboat) charter

The demise charter is more commonly called the bareboat charter. Time or voyage charter parties are contracts for the carriage of cargoes. The ship owner remains in control of the navigation and operation of the vessel and employment of the crew. The demise charter is a contract of possession and control of the vessel from the owner to another, similar to the lease of property. The key issue is control of the vessel. To recognize a demise charter, you must determine who has control of the vessel. If the owner retains control over the vessel to carry the cargo supplied by the charterer, then the charter is not demise. However, if the control of the vessel is surrendered to the charterer, with the Master and crew supplied and employed by the charterer, then you are dealing with a demise charter. The owner will only supply the vessel and cover the cost of its depreciation, insurance unless otherwise agreed, survey of the vessel for delivery on hire and the shipbroker's fee.

The charter hire is paid on a rate per summer deadweight and is payable each calendar month.

The demise charterer pays for the hiring of the Master and crew, wages, provisions and stores, maintenance and repairs, fuel, water and lubrication oils, all port charges, brokerage commissions on cargoes he arranges to carry and any cargo claims.

## 2.6.2    Time charter

Under a time charter, the owner allows the charterer the use of the cargo carrying capacity of the ship for a specific period of time. The owner maintains control of the navigation, crew, Master, hull and P&I insurance and all general matters connected with the operation of the vessel. The charterer will seek cargo employment for the vessel and will pay the owner a daily hire rate.

By obtaining full use of the vessel's cargo carrying and loading and discharge capacity, the charterer can order the vessel to proceed anywhere that is agreed in the trading limits clause of the time charter party. Therefore, the charterer is responsible for the fuel, port charges, repairs caused by cargo damages, payment of the hire and appointment of the load and discharge port agents.

The charterers in a time charter are interested in the vessel's speed as they will wish to maximize the number of voyages under the time charter. Other important aspects are fuel consumption, the vessel's deadweight cargo capacity and the vessel's class, which determines the cargo insurance costs.

Some of the general provisions of a time charter are the duration, trading limits, prohibited cargoes, safe port and berth clause, seaworthiness, vessel description, vessel speed and bunker consumption, hire rate, breakdown clauses, delivery and re-delivery time and place, performance of the officers and crew, cancellation clause and arbitration clause.

## 2.6.3    Voyage charter

The voyage charter is the most common charter used in tramp shipping. In this charter, the owner puts the vessel's cargo carrying capacity at the charterer's disposal for a full or part cargo from one named port or range of ports to another port or range of ports. The revenue earned by the ship owner is called freight. Freight is paid either on a lump sum basis or per ton of cargo.

> Under a voyage charter, the ship owner has the responsibility to present the vessel at the load port within the date range stipulated in the charter party. The range of dates are called 'laydays/cancelling' or 'laycan' for short. If the vessel does not arrive prior to the last day of the laydays, the voyage can be cancelled!

All the vessel operations and expenses are for the owner's account. The charterer's responsibility is to provide a specified cargo of a specific weight or volume at the port or ports stated in the charter party. The charterer must pay the freight and carry out repairs to any damage caused by the loading or discharge of cargo.

In most charter parties the charterer pays for the loading and discharge costs but, under liner terms, the ship owner pays for the loading and discharge of the cargoes.

Some of the general provisions of a voyage charter are vessel description, cargo volume, cargo description, loading and discharge ports, freight rate and lay time, which is the time allowed to the charterer to load and discharge cargo. Demurrage is the payment made to the owner by the charterer for exceeding the time allotted for loading and discharge.

Dispatch is the payment by the owner to the charterer for loading and discharging the vessel in a shorter period than stated in the charter party. Voyage charters have clauses covering port dues, wharfage and stevedoring, selection of the agents at load and discharge ports, commencement of laytime and tendering of notice of readiness.

## 2.7 The Freight Market

The freight market is not a physical place but a way of referring to the conditions existing on a particular trade. Freight is the amount charterers have to pay for moving their goods and it is affected by several variables, such as the supply and demand for vessels at a loading area and the trading patterns of the ship owners with available vessels. The trading pattern refers to the ability of the ship owner to load a cargo so that the discharge port is a place where he can likely obtain another cargo. The vessel size and the type of cargo affect the market demand. Other factors affecting market supply and demand include the arrival date of the vessel at the load port and the charterer's loading date requirements, the vessel's cost of operation and also the psychological and emotional state of the brokers and their principals. This final variable is the one most difficult to define as, like the stock market, the freight market can be affected by the pre and post-holiday blues, summer doldrums, international economics and events such as fear of wars, shortage of food or industrial material in a particular location or natural disasters.

# Chapter 3
## Shipbroking

Shipbrokers, acting as intermediaries, have proven themselves to be the most economical method for ship owners and potential ship charterers to come together for the negotiation of contracts of carriage.

The major centers of shipbroking today are London, Singapore and New York. However, due to the ease of communicating globally, shipbroking is done in many cities and countries around the world. A shipbroker can be found in almost every port of commercial importance.

A shipbroker can be an individual acting on his own or a large company with hundreds of brokers covering a variety of commodities moving in bulk.

Situated in London, the Baltic Exchange is the 'spiritual' home of shipbroking. The Baltic used to be a place with facilities similar to the New York Stock Exchange floor, providing a meeting place for brokers representing both shippers with cargoes requiring ships and brokers representing ship owners seeking employment. The Baltic remains a membership organization, which provides independent daily shipping market information and establishes and maintains professional shipbroking standards. Electronic communications allow brokers to match ships and cargoes without ever going near the Baltic.

In many countries there are no formal training programs required to become a shipbroker. Established shipbroking firms, with reputations for professionalism, make efforts to ensure their principals are being served by knowledgeable individuals. The UK based Institute of Chartered Shipbrokers (ICS) conducts an international teaching and testing program for the shipbroking profession. The brokers must comply with the minimum requirements that the Institute feels necessary to maintain standards that were set down decades ago by its founders. Membership of the Institute was not a strict requirement for shipbroking in England, but it was required to trade on the Baltic Exchange. Membership of both still provides status to their members even today and the ICS course is available globally.

Other educational offerings are also available in many countries. The internet has created many opportunities for online or distance learning courses.

In general, shipbrokers are persons with the ability to make deals and the contacts necessary to find two people to make a deal between.

Shipbroking service is provided by a system of worldwide intelligence about cargoes being moved and the location and availability of ships throughout the world seeking employment. The shipbroker's function can be stated as, specifically, to provide contacts, give advice to principals, conduct the negotiation between the ship owners and potential charterers on rates, terms and conditions for performance and to prepare the final contract (charter party) and present it to both parties.

# 3.1 Types of Shipbrokers

## 3.1.1 Owner's broker

A ship owner appoints a broker or brokers to represent him in seeking advice and information as to the location of cargoes to be moved. This broker is authorized by the ship owner to advise other brokers with cargoes of the vessel's name, description, location and dates available. Having found a cargo matching the ship's locations, dimensions and freight rates being offered, the owner will instruct the broker to commence negotiations with the party representing the cargo interest.

## 3.1.2 Charterer's broker

A shipper seeking a vessel to move his cargo from one port to another will inform his broker or brokers of his cargo movement schedule, the volume of cargo to be moved and the amount of freight on offer. This broker, in turn, will contact ship owners, or other brokers representing ship owners, for advice on the availability and position of ships and the dimensions suitable for carriage of the cargo on offer.

## 3.1.3 Tanker brokers

These shipbrokers specialize in liquid bulk ships and cargoes. In the tanker branch of shipping, one broker acts as the intermediary between charterer and owner.

## 3.1.4 Cable brokers

This is a slightly dated term for large broking houses with offices in a number of major centers. It refers to the days when cables were used for communication. By having offices worldwide, one company can cover all markets throughout the entire industry. Each broker's office issues lists of cargoes being shipped and seeking vessels. The same office might also issue 'positions of vessels' – the lists of ships and their dimensions with dates of availability. At the end of each day's business, the broker issues a list of fixtures (concluded contracts) reported for that day and sends this information to all the broker's branch offices worldwide, for distribution to the charterers and ship owners served by each office. Employing a large worldwide broker increases the scope of opportunity of the charterer and ship owner of fixing cargo and ships at the desired rate. Today, shipbrokers large and small use integrated computer networks and the internet, which allows them to talk to each other and to clients on screen in real time, should they choose, and even to negotiate live.

# 3.2    The Freight Market

The freight market indicates the trend or state of balance of the number of vessels and cargoes available for carriage at a given time and place throughout the world. That balance of supply and demand is reflected in the freight rates offered to ship owners under specific conditions in specific commodity trades that move in bulk on tramp vessels.

To understand the full scope of market conditions and developing trends, and in turn to give advice to ship owners and charterers, the broker must have a sound knowledge of the following disciplines: trade routes, ships and ship design, ports, cargoes, ship operations, economics, world events and strikes. The ramifications of any of these alone or combined, may affect the freight market and the potential success for the broker's principal.

While acting on a principal's behalf in the freight market, the broker must maintain the following concepts and rules:

**First and foremost is:** "Our word is our bond". This is the fundamental principle of trust that binds all shipbrokers. By this phrase, shipbrokers worldwide maintain the professional virtue that, in all negotiations on behalf of their principal, no one broker will lie to another to mislead deliberately the other broker and principal. Furthermore, no one broker, having had authority to enter into negotiations that result in a fixture, will deny having done so in order to enter other negotiations to gain a larger commission for himself.

**Second:** The broker will keep both owners or charterers, i.e. whichever he represents in any given negotiation, continually updated of changes in market conditions that affect their business.

**Third:** Brokers will only act within the scope of specific authority granted to them by their principals.

**Fourth:** The broker will always keep his principal's best interest in mind, foremost above earning his commission, and never allow a principal to unknowingly enter into a bad business venture.

**Fifth:** The broker will never withhold information from the principal, or release information about the principal's business that has been given to the broker in strict confidence.

For their efforts, shipbrokers earn a commission, which is a percentage of the freight. The commission is usually 1.25% to each broker in dry cargo or 2.5% to the single broker in tankers. It is important to note that commission is negotiable, and can vary from one fixture to another. If negotiations to the fixture fail, the broker earns nothing.

In addition to the functions of market trends and charter negotiation, shipbrokers' services are broken down into the following areas of service to the shipping industry:

- Charter brokerage
- sale and purchase brokerage
- port agency.

Charter brokerage has already been explained.

## Sale and purchase

This brokerage service specializes in arranging for the sale and purchase of vessels, and occasionally assists in the financing of the purchase or building of a new vessel.

## Port agency

The port agency function of the shipbroking business goes hand in hand with providing the shipping industry with the full services it requires. Brokers can arrange the sale and purchase of an owner's vessel, provide it with cargoes to load and, when the vessel calls at the broker's port, the broker can attend to the owner's and ship's business of husbandry and port services and assist the Master with operational aspects of the cargo loading or discharge.

# Chapter 4
## Tramp Ship Agency Practice

## 4.1 Port Agency Companies

There are many companies worldwide that provide ship agency services as their sole business. Most shipbrokers no longer provide port agency services as an adjunct to their business. Today, newer, well-established ship agency companies may provide port agency in one port, or many ports within a nation or region. Many of these large agency companies, with offices and staff in many ports worldwide, can also service both liner and tramp vessels. These companies offer both charterers and ship owners coordination between ports, standardized financial reporting and a standard agency fee at all ports. The choice of agent depends upon the preferences of the principal, and the attributes that define these choices are explored in Chapter 12. Competition among agents is fierce at all levels.

## 4.2 Tramp Agency Operation

The size of the agency depends upon the number of tramp vessels serviced per year and whether the agency also acts as a loading broker or a general agent for the liner company/companies it services.

The tramp agency staff will usually include an operations manager, boarding agents, secretarial staff and accounting staff. Remuneration is based on the revenue gained from the agency fee, expenses and special services. The profit earning ability of the tramp agency is based upon the revenue generated in excess of the overhead cost required to satisfactorily service principals' needs.

The operations manager is the coordinator of the three facets of tramp agency: pre-vessel arrival, port call and after sailing service.

# 4.3    Pre-arrival

Both owners and charterers need to know estimated port costs to load or discharge any specific cargo on a particular vessel. Additionally, the principals need to know port conditions, berth restrictions on the ship's size and berth availability, all prior to or concurrent with charter party negotiations. The operations manager, as quickly as possible, will provide the principal with the estimated port charges together with port conditions and berth conditions that will affect the lay time or other charter party obligations of the principal.

Once negotiations to charter a specific vessel to load or discharge at the agent's port have been concluded, the owner or charterer will notify the agent of the vessel's arrival and any special details of the charter party. The notification to the agent, whether in writing or by telephone, is called the agency appointment.

Except for emergencies, the majority, if not all, of the principals' and agents' correspondence is in writing, usually by email.

The operations manager's written acknowledgment of the agency appointment will include gratitude for the appointment, an update of the port cost estimates, current and forecasted port conditions and the preliminary prospects for loading or discharging, berthing and sailing. The berthing, loading or discharge and vessel sailing prospects will be updated continuously, or at least once a day, by the agents. The acknowledgment of the agency appointment to the ship owner will include the agent's banking information, to allow the owner to remit the required estimated port cost to the agent in advance of the ship's arrival.

The Master will begin sending the agents the daily ETA update. This information is forwarded to the owner, charterer's representative, the shippers or consignees and their terminals or stevedores.

The operations manager coordinates with the shippers or consignees for the berthing of the vessel and relays this information to the agency's principal. The accuracy of information required by all parties connected with the vessel is crucial to the performance of the agent's primary function, which is to expedite the ship's port call.

Expediting the ship's port call requires coordination of the vessel's cargo operations and husbandry matters in an economical and timely manner, thereby permitting the vessel to return to, or commence, her voyage or get back into the market for the next cargo.

Before vessel arrival, the operations manager will communicate with the Master, advising estimated berthing, cargo commencement and what is required to prepare the vessel in advance for cargo operations. He will also inform the Master of the local government requirements for port entry, including preparation of port security compliance, customs forms and formal notices of arrival to government authorities. Most importantly, he will provide the Master with a description of the berth and any port and berth restrictions. This is needed to allow the Master to raise any concern that the ship will not be kept within the safe berth clause of the charter party.

Concurrent with the information to cargo interests and principals, the agent will notify the appropriate port organizations, such as the port authority, harbor master, national security, customs, immigration, health, coast guard, linemen, tug companies and pilots, of the vessel arrival in accordance with each organization's regulations and requirements.

Coordination and sufficient notice to all is crucial as failure to give timely notices could delay vessel turnaround and cause the principals to incur charter party loss of time or penalties from government authorities.

### 4.3.1    Pre-arrival functions

- Advise the ship owner of estimated port costs. For loading, obtain confirmation the cargo is ready and obtain a draft copy of the B/L to present to the owner so that they can review and approve the terms and conditions. If the vessel is going to discharge cargo, inform the owner whether the receivers will present the original B/L to the Master or submit a letter of indemnity (LOI) for the release of cargo without presentation of OBL

- keep the ship owner, shippers/receivers, charterers and terminal advised of the vessel's ETA, berthing and cargo operation prospects daily

- provide a line-up of the ships scheduled at the terminal

- accept and forward cargo instructions to the Master and owner

- ensure the Master is aware of all port and terminal conditions so the vessel is able to proceed to, remain at and depart from any berth while remaining safely afloat at all times

- coordinate the presence of cargo surveyors and government agencies for the ship's arrival

- arrange and/or attend to customs clearance and all other services pertaining to the vessel's movements while entering port, during stay and leaving port

- arrange contracts for pilotage, towage, stevedoring, tallying and ancillary services.

## 4.4    The Port Call

As the vessel arrives into port, the operations manager will arrange for one of the agency's boarding agents to attend the vessel after anchoring or berthing. The boarding agent's function is to coordinate the government authorities' duties with the Master at the preliminary boarding and inspection of the vessel and to ensure that the Master completes the required government forms to the authorities' satisfaction. They will also assist in the immigration interviews of the ship's crew and instruct the Master to have a ship officer join the customs officers' inspection of the vessel's cargo. Once the preliminary boarding has been satisfied, the boarding agent will sit with the Master and review the husbandry requirements for the vessel and crew. The agent also reviews, with the Master, the shifting, berthing and cargo operations schedule.

In general, the agent does all the things that the Master is unable to do because of his inability to leave the vessel or because there is insufficient time; i.e. arranging vessel repairs, ship chandlers, crew repatriations, transporting crew and attending the customs house to enter and clear the vessel.

Provisioning is best left to the ship chandler and the Master and chief engineer will deal directly with suppliers rather than using the agent as an intermediary. Technical descriptions and visual analysis of spare parts can become misconstrued if described by an intermediary.

Once the arrival formalities are completed, the agent assists the Master to tender the notice of readiness (NOR) in accordance with the terms of the governing charter party agreement and instructions from the ship owner.

The NOR is the vessel's notice to the charterers, shippers or consignees of vessel's readiness to load or discharge in accordance with the charter party. The NOR is the foremost responsibility of the agents once the vessel has arrived. The Master will authorize the agent to present the NOR to the charterers, shippers, receivers or their agents in writing. This can be accomplished by hand delivery, requiring the recipient to sign the NOR as received, or the agent can tender the NOR via email, telex or fax. This is very important as the NOR will commence lay time in accordance with the charter party which, in turn, will impact when the charterer will have to complete cargo operations before incurring demurrage charges.

The agent will notify the principals of the ship's arrival, the amount of fuel, diesel and water on board, the time the NOR was tendered and accepted and prospects for start and finish of cargo operations. This must be done without delay, regardless of the day or the time of the ship's arrival in port.

During the vessel's port stay, the operations manager will liaise with the stevedores, terminal and the Master to ensure the vessel's progress is proceeding as scheduled. The operations manager will keep the principal advised, once or twice daily, of when the cargo operations can be expected to end so the vessel can sail. The boarding agents will visit the vessel at least once per day, or more often if necessary, to meet the Master and to assist him with any cargo problems or to accept additional requirements needing attention.

On completion of the cargo operations, the boarding agent will see the vessel off. At the time of sailing, the agent will present the Master with the completed Statement of Facts for his signature. This document confirms that all times for the vessel's port stay, including maneuvers and cargo operations, are correct. The agent will obtain from the Master the final times for the completion of the cargo operations, the ship's sailing conditions and the ETA at the next port. The sailing details are immediately sent to the principal.

### 4.4.1 Port call functions

- Attend to the ship on arrival in port. After the vessel is cleared by government authorities and cargo surveys have been completed, the agent will receive the NOR from the Master and present it to the shippers/receivers, terminal and charterers. The agent will report the arrival conditions and commencement of cargo operation details to the owner and charterers

- supervise operations and ensure efficient dispatch of the vessel

- inform charterers and owner, on a daily basis, of ongoing cargo operations including an estimate of completion and vessel sailing

- be present on board on arrival and sailing, on commencement and completion of cargo operations and during undocking for every berth

- attend the ship at least once daily and whenever requested by the Master, owner or charterers

- prepare and issue cargo documents

- attend to husbandry requirements

- attend to additional services in connection with claims, consular authorities, etc., as required

- if loading cargo, present to the Master and owner a draft B/L to review the terms and conditions and approve the use of this B/L. The agent should also obtain a letter from the Master authorizing the agents to sign the B/L on his behalf. This is needed in the event that the B/L is not ready for the Master's signature, or if changes need to be made after the ship sails.

The agent is to hold the B/L until the owner authorizes its release to the shippers.

# 4.5 After Sailing Service

This aspect of the agency attendance is just as important as the previous two. During this period, the agent will wait for the owner's authority to release the original B/Ls to the shippers. The agent should never release the B/Ls without specific written instructions to do so from the owner. The agent will also have obtained the Master's written authorization to sign B/Ls on his behalf. This is done if B/Ls are not ready for the Master to sign prior to sailing or if they require amendments to satisfy the charter party terms or to include in the B/L the actual quantity of cargo loaded. As soon as possible after the ship sails, the agent prepares the statement of facts, NOR, Master's protests, surveyor reports and timesheets covering the vessel's cargo operations. This information and documentation is needed by the principal immediately after the vessel's departure. The agent will send the documents by email or by fax. The original documents will be sent to the principal by courier. These documents are required for the finalization of the voyage charges. They are also required if demurrage has been incurred; i.e. where the charterer must make additional payments for failure to load or discharge the vessel within the stipulated amount of time allowed by the charter party. In the tanker market, some charterers insert a time bar clause for demurrage claims of 45 or 60 days after the vessel's completion of cargo operations. An agent should coordinate with the ship owner/principal to assure that the ship owner has all the information needed to assert a timely demurrage claim.

Finally, the agent will render the disbursement account, which is an accurate statement of how the agent disbursed the funds advanced to the agent by the principal. The general rule is for the disbursement account to be rendered as soon as possible after the vessel's departure. Vendor bills are usually received by the agent within 30 days of rendering service. The agents will pay all bills and forward to the owner a list of the services rendered together with the supporting invoices. This rendering of disbursements against advanced funds has always been a major problem in the relationship between owners and their agents. If the final disbursement account is not timely or is not well organized, the ship operations and accounting staff of the ship owner will become frustrated. The disbursement account is the last impression left by a ship's agent with his principal and care should be taken to assure it is accurate, timely and complete.

### 4.5.1    **After sailing functions**

- Immediately upon the completion of cargo operations, the agent should report the quantity of cargo loaded or discharged and the results of surveys

- within the same day as the ship's departure, the agent should forward the statement of facts and other cargo documents to the ship owner and charterer

- sign and release the B/Ls for cargo loaded in accordance with the ship owner's and Master's authority and the charterer's instructions

- submit final disbursement account to the ship owner, within 30 days if possible.

# 4.6    Functions of Agency Staff Members

To provide competent port agency service and encourage repeat business, the agency will require certain minimum staffing.

### 4.6.1    Operations manager

All decisions originate from the operations manager, who ensures that the boarding agents are fully prepared prior to boarding any vessel, giving them full knowledge of all the Master and crew requirements and the schedule of cargo operations. As the boarding agents are usually in the field, they have little time when they return to the office to coordinate the next vessel's arrival into port. Therefore, all the pre-arrival and part of the coordination work falls upon the operations manager. Depending on the volume of vessels and the availability of boarding agents in the office, the operations manager will delegate instructions for vessel preparation to the boarding agents. The operations manager will usually be the first point of contact with the principal.

### 4.6.2    Boarding agents

The reputation of the ship agency within the port and with the principals hinges upon the boarding agents. Because tramps arrive at all times of day and night, weekends and holidays included, these people must be energetic, organized and dedicated. The boarding agents are the salesmen for the agency. Their enthusiasm and concern for detail are of major importance because, no matter how competent the operations manager, the boarding agents are the physical representatives of the company. The boarding agents must be perceptive enough to sense a developing problem and, together with the Master and operations manager, take the appropriate action to protect the principal's interest.

Boarding agents must always show the capacity to make the extra effort to please the Master, who is the on-site representative of both the owner and the charterer.

### 4.6.3    Accounting staff

The accounting department covers both the pre-arrival and after sailing segments of a ship call. When the principal remits funds to the agent's bank, the accounting department traces the receipt and advises the operations manager. The accountant's ability to trace funds through international banking is very important. Rendering of the disbursement account with supporting documentation is the primary function of the accountant. The principal's last communication with the agents is in the presentation of the disbursement account, so a sloppy and inaccurate account, without sufficient detail or transparency, can negate whatever good efforts were made by the operations staff.

The timeliness of rendering of disbursements is important. The disbursement account should be prepared and forwarded to the owner within 30 to 40 days of the ship's departure.

# Chapter 5
## Defining Tramp Agency and the Scope of Services Provided

------------------------------------------------

This chapter defines tramp ship agencies and describes the services they provide to ship owners and charterers.

The movement of a particular cargo on a specific vessel from one port to another involves many participants: the shipper, the charterer, the shipbroker, the ship owner and the consignee. Each may have a representative or agent at the port of loading and discharge. The agent of each participant will have specific authority from the principal to protect the principal's interests in the venture. The agency services rendered will differ in each participant's case. This differentiation of agency representation can be confusing to newcomers to tramp shipping if they do not fully understand who each agent is working for, the nature of the agency business and the scope of the agent's authority.

Agency is the name given to the legal relationship that arises when two parties enter into an agreement where one of the parties, called the agent, agrees to represent or act for the other, called the principal, subject to the principal's right to control the agent's conduct concerning the matters entrusted to him.

The shipping industry has two categories of agency: (i) a general or booking agent usually employed in liner shipping and (ii) a special agent, mostly used in tramp shipping.

## 5.1    General Agent

Liner shipping serves specific ports between two or more geographic areas, called a trade route. Liner ships that call at these ports advertise their sailing dates to all potential shippers on the trade route.

It would not be economically feasible for the liner company to maintain an office and staff in each of the ports in all of the countries in the geographic area that it serves. Therefore, a general agent is usually employed.

The general agent is an agent with authority from a principal to act on all matters concerning a particular trade. The general agent's authority is established by a formal written agreement, defining the agent's authority to act on behalf of the principal on a continuing basis for a specific period of time. The cancellation notices and date of the contract are also detailed within the agreement.

In liner shipping, the agent's remuneration is usually a percentage of the outbound freight booked by the agent and a percentage of the freight value of the inbound cargo. The agent also earns revenue from several other services, such as container control, ship husbandry, trucking, inland logistics and stevedoring.

A general agent in tramp shipping can take many forms. In some instances, the general tramp agent may represent a tramp owner, whereby the agent has authority to seek cargo, disburse funds, select and appoint sub-agents and make operations decisions without seeking the owner's authority first. The general agent may also have authority to enter into or conclude charter party negotiations. This type of agent may act as the owner's representative in a geographic area. Although their legal relationship to each other and to all third parties is as the 'owner's local office', these agents will still want to assure that they act within the legal boundaries of agency law to limit their own direct liability.

In some cases, a general tramp agent may represent a charterer, rather than the ship owner. In this situation, a charterer may voyage charter a vessel with the right to nominate the port agents to be appointed by the ship owner. The charterer may fix the charter party with an option of any port in a geographical area. In these cases, the charterer needs the general agent to coordinate all sub-agents in the port range. A good example would be an oil trader who is not sure at which port the cargo it has chartered the ship to carry will be sold. It instructs the owner to have the ship proceed to New York for orders and to appoint a specific New York agent that the voyage charterer will nominate. The ship owner is obligated to appoint the New York agent, even though the ship may eventually be ordered to another US port where the New York agent will appoint a sub-agent with the owner's authority to do so. The advantage to the charterer is time saved issuing standard operating instructions on short notice to unfamiliar port agents. The charterer's general agent will issue to the sub-agent both the charterer's and owner's instructions regarding communication, documentation and cargo operations. The charterer's general agent will, usually, supervise the sub-agent on behalf of the charterer and owner with respect to compliance with instructions and issuing cargo load or discharge orders. This agent may also coordinate sending the ship owner's previously advanced funds to local agents to avoid delays getting advanced disbursements into the local agent's possession.

The advantage of the tramp general agent to both owner and charterer is more rapid coordination of the vessel's movement, service consistency at all ports and the quick movement of funds among agents at different ports. The general agent provides both an owner and charterer with established operating, communication and documentation procedures.

Nevertheless, the general agent's authority is not without limit. Regardless of the relationship, the prudent general agent should always seek the principal's ratification of any action taken by the general agent in the event of an extraordinary occurrence.

The tramp general agent's remuneration will depend upon the principal and the service performed. A tramp general agent for a ship owner might be paid an annual lump sum retainer plus a broker's commission for cargoes fixed, plus a fee and expenses for each ship supervised. Another remuneration option is when the ship owner pays the tramp general agent on an 'as needed' basis. In this case, the general agent is paid an agency fee, plus administration expenses for each port call in the agent's port, or when supervising a sub-agent on behalf of the principal. The compensation can take the form of a combination of one, two or all the above methods of remuneration.

The charterer's tramp general agent can also be paid by a lump sum annual retainer, broker's commission and supervisory fees. If a supervisory fee is paid by the voyage charterer to the general agent, the general agent is paid a port agency fee for services rendered during the usual port call services to the owner.

To summarize, the tramp general agent usually has a contractual relationship covering a specified period of time. The general agent's authority is continuous beyond one port and one vessel. The general agent, similar to the liner general agent, is likely to have authority to seek cargo or suitable vessels for the owner or charterer. Although the tramp general agent's operational authority is expanded beyond the normal port agent's, the authority is unlikely to be unlimited or infinite. There will more likely be an agreed limit up to which the tramp general agent is free to act without specific additional authority.

# 5.2    Special Agent

The tramp vessel operator is not limited to a particular trade route, fixed schedule or category of cargoes. Instead, the tramp vessel operator may trade in bulk or general cargoes wherever available. Consequently, the tramp vessel operator will have vessels calling in a wide range of possible ports worldwide.

In this trade, agency services are by definition required only on an occasional basis, depending on the ports stipulated in each new charter party. This type of agent is therefore often described as a 'special' agent and is only required for one vessel calling at a named port with a specific cargo under a distinct charter, usually for one voyage.

The special agent can, therefore, be defined as an agent having authority to act for a special occasion or purpose, where the agent's authority is limited. Once the ship's business at the agent's port has been concluded, the agent no longer has authority to take any other actions on behalf of the principal unless the principal contacts the agent with new authority covering a continuation of the voyage or because of a new situation or a second port call for the same ship returning to the port at a later date.

Within the scope of work of a special agent in tramp ship agency, there exists a subdivision of agency functions depending on who the agent is representing in a specific instance. There can be as many agents appointed to one cargo operation as there are different principals, each with a specific interest to protect. Each of the ship owners, charterers, shippers, receivers or time charterers, if that is the case, may employ their own agent to protect their respective interests. Unless each has a complete understanding of special agency and how it interacts with the agents of other principals who have differing interests in the same venture, confusion can result in damage to or embarrassment of their principal.

## 5.3    The Right to Select the Port Agent

A charter party clause dedicated to agency matters, covering the assignment of agents at load and discharge port, provides control of the agency appointment. In some charter parties, the charterer will negotiate with the ship owner for the right to nominate agents at the load or discharge port.

## 5.4    Charterer's Nominated Agents

The governing charter party agreement will often contain a clause dealing with the nomination of agents at the load and/or discharge port. Often, the charterer has the right to nominate the agent, who is then formally appointed by the ship owner. The ship owner is also responsible for payment of the agent's fees and expenses, along with port charges. The agent will also be the agent of record with port authorities and government officials. The agent is obligated to serve and protect the ship owner's interests and, although nominated by the charterer, at all times remains under the control of the ship owner.

### 5.4.1    Owner or time charterer's agent

This is the agent appointed where the charter party allows the owner or time charterer the right to appoint their agents of choice at the load and discharge ports for the purposes of national or port security requirements, customs clearance, Master and crew requirements, port disbursements, arranging tugs and pilotage, arranging cargo operations and all other matters that the ship owner or time charterer would carry out if they had an office with employees at the port.

## 5.4.2    Protecting or supervisory agent

In this instance, the owner or charterer appoints an agent to protect their interest when, under the charter party, the vessel is consigned to another agent. If the charter party calls for owner's agents, the charterer may nevertheless appoint a protecting or supervisory agent to protect the charterer's individual interests at the load or discharge port. The same applies to ship owners, time charterers and voyage charterers. This agent is not usually the agent of record with the port authorities and government officials.

## 5.4.3    The husbandry agent

This term describes an agent appointed by the ship owner to attend only to non-cargo matters, specifically those matters concerning vessel crew, repairs, supplies and provisioning and Classification Society surveys.

The following hypothetical voyage will help illustrate the different role of each of the above-defined special agents.

Consider a vessel and voyage where the owner, charterer and time charterer each employ their own agents.

The principals are as follows:

- The tanker 'Sea Star' is owned by Sea Nav Ltd of London.

- The Iowa Oil Co has time chartered the 'Sea Star' for a period 5 years.

- The New York Fuel Oil Supply Co has voyage chartered the 'Sea Star' for a single-voyage charter with Iowa Oil Co to carry oil from Venezuela to New York.

- New York Fuel Oil Supply has sold the oil cargo to Con Edison, a New York utility company.

In accordance with the charter party between New York Fuel, as voyage charterer, and Iowa Oil Co, as ship operators, New York Fuel has the right to nominate the port agents that Iowa must appoint at the discharge port.

New York Fuel nominated Joe Ship Agency ('Joe Agency'). Iowa appoints Joe Agency to attend the vessel's call at New York.

Iowa has never worked with Joe Agency before, so appoints its own protecting agents, Ted Shipping, to supervise the actions of Joe Agency and the cargo operations from the time chartered operator's point of interest.

The actual owners of 'Sea Star', Sea Nav of London, have never worked with Joe Agency or Ted Shipping before, so they appoint Mac Agencies to attend to the Master, crew and vessel husbandry requirements.

Joe Agency, being the consigned agent of record, receives an agency appointment from Iowa and requests funds to cover port charges, tugs and customs clearances of the vessel and his agency fees. Shifting to and from Con Edison's berth is co-coordinated by Joe Agency, on behalf of Iowa, as per the authority Joe received from Iowa to handle those matters.

Joe Agency, at the same time, contacts New York Fuels for instructions as to where and to whom the vessel is to deliver the cargo. In this case the consignee is Con Edison. Joe Agency will inform Iowa, the ship operator, of the charterer's intention and the name of the receivers. He will also ask the receivers to present the original B/L so as to obtain the release of the cargo. Joe Agency will confirm to Iowa when the B/L is in hand.

To protect Iowa's interest as the time charter operator, the request for port charges by Joe Agency is given through Iowa's agent, Ted Shipping. Ted Shipping will receive the money from Iowa and will then remit the funds to Joe Agency. Ted Shipping will also see that the vessel is put into a safe berth at ConEdison, as coordinated by Joe Agency. In general, Ted Shipping will protect Iowa's interests by seeing that Joe Agency's actions with Iowa's vessel are safe and in accordance with the charter party terms, so that Iowa's interests are not adversely prejudiced by New York Fuel's agent, Joe Agency, which may adversely affect Iowa's responsibility to Sea Nav under the time charter.

Iowa's agent, Ted Shipping, will also report to Iowa details about the port operations in addition to the information being provided by Joe Agency. This allows Iowa to have their own point of view that the ship's time used and terminal operation are within the charter party agreement. This includes comparison of the statement of facts and researching any discrepancy or concern Iowa may have about the port operations.

The third agent is Mac. Mac is the vessel owner's husbandry agent, appointed by Sea Nav to arrange crew medical needs, Master requirements such as food, voyage repairs, cash advances to the crew and other ship-owning related matters. Mac will take no action in the cargo operations unless a problem arises that will affect Sea Nav's contractual obligation with Iowa within the terms of the time charter, such as vessel performance.

From this example, it can be seen that each party with an interest in the vessel and voyage can have an agent representing and protecting their interests based upon their respective contractual obligations.

# 5.5    Hub Agent

A hub agent is similar to a general agent. This type of agency service was developed during the mid-1990s by large ship agencies at the encouragement of oil companies holding fleets of owned and time chartered tankers. The main goals of the oil companies were (i) to reduce the cost of having staff handling disbursement accounts, (ii) to reduce the large amounts of cash flow out to agents worldwide, (iii) to consolidate communications systems, and (iv) to create consistency in port agency services.

A hub agent can serve any ship owner, charterer or commodity; although it is oil companies and tanker owners that tend to prefer this type of service. Oil companies generally have routine sources of crude oil which is shipped on owned, time chartered or voyage chartered tankers to company-owned refineries.

A hub agent generally has offices in the ports from which the oil company regularly sources their crude oil, as well as at ports of destination where the refineries are located. Often, but not always, a hub agent may have offices in ports that service the oil companies clients for the purposes of handling refined products. The hub system has become particularly useful for those oil companies that have moved away from ship owning.

When chartering ships on a voyage basis, oil companies can take advantage of the clause in the charter party permitting charterer's nomination of the agent by nominating their preferred agents. This will result in the owner appointing the oil company's hub agent or sub-agent, who is familiar with the oil company's operating systems, facilities, personnel, and quality control criteria.

The hub agency system can also be molded to fit the needs of the principals. The primary service of a hub agent is a software system that can be easily accessed or, in some cases, be integrated into the oil companies' own systems. The hub agent software provides consistency in communications, electronic transfer of documentation and disbursement account management.

Examples of hub agency services are:

- Live web-based access to port operations and disbursement accounting
- single bank account for all worldwide fund transfers for disbursement accounts
- an established agency network of the hub agency offices and sub-agents and continued employment of agents, preferred by the principal, who become the sub-agents
- jointly established port agency operating procedures at all ports
- regional hub offices that appoint agents to supervise local agent services and disburse funds for port costs
- port cost analysis to negotiate volume discounts for the principal from local service providers and vendors
- electronic storage of port documents.

There are many other services a hub agent can provide at the request of the principal. In most instances, the local port agency operations are in direct contact with the ship operator, although the local hub office will be copied in on communications and will intervene when necessary. The local agent's performance and the ship's operation remain in the control of the principal. The hub is a third party service that the principal uses for outsourcing disbursement account management, port cost analysis, agency networking and supervision, document storage and communication systems.

The hub agent is under contract to the principal and can provide all or part of the services outlined above. The hub agent, in some cases, can issue instructions to the local agents on behalf of the principal. However, the local agent must recognize that the hub agent is a third party outsource provider to the oil company or ship owner, and not the principal.

The principal requests the local agent to coordinate funding for the port call with the hub agent acting on behalf of the principal. The hub agent will, in most cases, not be liable for the principal's debts. The local agent's authority to act is taken directly from the principal and they should not take orders from the hub agent unless the principal clearly confirms, in writing, that the hub agent has full authority to issue instructions for the principal.

In the same context, the hub agent will seek to negotiate reduced port costs for the principal. This will include the local agent's compensation. The local agent can offer a discount of their agency fees for the principal, but the agent should not be obligated to do so for the hub agent.

## 5.6    Other Outsource Agency Services

In addition to the hub services, there are firms that provide disbursement account management accounting services only, with no supporting owned ship agent network.

These firms will relay the principal's agency appointment to the agent with instructions on how to present estimated port costs and the final disbursement account. In a similar manner to the hub agent's financial function, the outsource accounting firm will compare the local agent's port estimate against previous port calls, perhaps ask for explanations, and then inform the owner when the estimated request passes the analyses by the disbursement management firm. The disbursement management firm will ask the principal for authority to remit funds to the agent. The agent will present the final disbursement account to the disbursement management accounting service, which will review, analyze and recommend settlement to the owner. The principal will issue the confirmation to remit settlement to the agents. In the majority of cases, the disbursement management accounting firm is not the principal and is not responsible for the principal's debts. Any disagreement on port costs or agency compensation should be discussed directly with the principal and not the disbursement management accounting firm.

The disbursement management accounting firm provides principals with staff relief of disbursement analysis, faster turnaround of cash flow to local ports and consolidated statements of accounts and banking services. The benefit to the local agent is usually a faster turnaround of their disbursement account settlements. The disadvantage to the local agent is that, if the accounting firm has a high staff turnover, there is the potential to be repeatedly asked the same questions on certain port costs.

Neither the hub agent nor service firms should be accepted as being the principal by the local agent.

In all cases, the local agents will have a direct relationship with the principal.

# Chapter 6
## The Law of Agency

## 6.1    The Relationship of Agency

Ship owners cannot have their own offices in every port to look after the needs of their vessels as they transport cargo worldwide. Instead, the ship agent steps in to fulfill that need through the creation of an agency relationship with the ship owner or other operator of the vessel. In an agency relationship, the principal authorizes the agent to deal with third parties on behalf of the principal and in some cases to legally bind the principal. In a sense, the actions of the agent are deemed to be the actions of the principal.

While an agency agreement is a legal relationship where the agent agrees to act on behalf of the principal, subject to the principal's authority, agency law varies from country to country. Further, the law is often changing and the current understanding of local law may be changed by subsequent court rulings. Therefore, it is important that agents, if confronted with a possible legal matter, consult with their insurer, company lawyer or outside legal adviser.

 **This book has used US Law for the purposes of describing various legal principles relating to agency.**

The law of agency varies throughout the world. The student of agency must understand his national and local laws to fully evaluate the risk of agency liability. Although this book is written from the US perspective, the text will raise questions for you to consider in your own situation.

Under US Law, remuneration alone does not determine whether an agency relationship exists. Actual consent between agent and principal is the key factor. In some instances, the agent may act on behalf of the principal gratuitously (i.e. without remuneration) and still maintain the power to bind the principal to third parties. This is particularly true in tramp agency, where a major principal may ask the agent to perform a minor task as a favor; e.g. arrange to meet crew members at the local airport for flight layover, to collect freight or coordinate bunker delivery.

The situation of acting on behalf of the principal without payment is an illustration of the fiduciary nature of agency. A fiduciary relationship is one of trust and the agent is duty-bound to protect and preserve the property and earnings of his principal. In general, the agent agrees to act for the benefit of his principal.

## 6.2    The Creation of Agency

In the well-known legal treatise, *'Scrutton on Charter Parties'*, agency is described under English law as follows:

> *"a person professing to act as agent can bind his principal if the principal has done the following:*
>
> 1.   *Given the agent actual authority to make a contract.*
>
> 2.   *Placed the agent in a position of apparent authority and allowed him to represent the principal as having such authority.*
>
> 3.   *If the agent has performed a task for the principal without the principal's express authority, the principal subsequently ratifies the agent's actions".*

The relationship between principal and agent is created when the principal demonstrates, in an express or implied manner, that he wishes the agent to act on his behalf in some specific capacity. Without the principal's demonstration giving consent to the agent to act, authority for the agent to act will not exist. It is not necessary for the agent to express to the principal consent to act. In practice, however, in tramp ship agency, the agent will generally acknowledge the principal's demonstration when he appoints the agent to attend a ship.

The principal's appointment of the agent can be expressed or implied. In tramp shipping, a principal's express demonstration to grant the authority will be in writing or by a telephone call to the agent. In an express appointment, the principal will outline for the agent the exact nature of the agency appointment and give specific authority in those matters where the principal requires the agent's special action.

Implied authority may be found where the agent must take action without having specific, express authority, but where the agent must still act so as to comply with the instructions given by the principal appointing the agent. An example of implied authority would be where the agent must apply and purchase a customs bond or berth usage application to allow the vessel port entry and berthing permission, even though the principal's original authority did not specifically identify these activities. Under this illustration, the agent may nevertheless be deemed to have implied authority to perform these tasks, since they are essential to carrying out the principal's business.

## 6.3    Agency by Necessity

On occasion, a tramp ship agent is confronted with a situation where he must act because of an emergency situation to protect his principal, even though the agent may not have express authority from the principal to take that action. In these cases, an agency relationship is said to arise by necessity.

In general agents must adhere to the principle of special agency. Special agents are those appointed for a particular vessel, usually under a single voyage charter. The special agency is not continuous and, therefore, ceases to exist after the vessel sails and the principal's port expenses have been paid by the agents.

The agent, having been appointed by the principal, has the authority to enter into contractual relations with third parties on behalf of the principal. Therefore, the agent may procure for his principal tug-boat services, linesmen, pilots and stevedores when he is instructed to operate the principal's vessel within the port for the purpose of loading and/or discharging cargo. Should an extraordinary occurrence take place, or an unexpected expenditure be required, the special agent would be required to obtain additional authority from the principal to take action on his behalf.

In the event of an extraordinary occurrence or expenditure, where the agent is unable to communicate with the principal, the agent's authority may be derived by necessity. Authority by necessity is different from express or implied authority.

Authority derived out of necessity, due to lack of communication with the principal, is less likely to arise with modern communications such as the mobile telephone, hand-held email communication and text messaging. However, with principals located anywhere in the world, there can be instances when a principal is unreachable. In such cases, authority is derived from the necessity to take action to protect the principal's interests.

An illustration of an extraordinary occurrence is a tanker having an oil spill requiring notification of the owner's P&I Club, or a maritime accident where the ship must be towed to a lay berth or dry dock immediately.

In each of these instances, the agent endeavors to protect the owner's interest. Of course, the agent would be wise to also take steps to protect his own interests as well by obtaining authority from the Master for the actions he takes. The Master is always the agent for the owner or the time charterer as he is the direct representative of the ship owner and, in most cases, has the authority to take whatever actions are necessary to protect the ship and cargo on board.

# 6.4　Ratification by Principals

Ratification occurs when the agent takes action without having authority, but the principal subsequently grants the authority or shows acceptance of the agent's actions. Ratification, therefore, entails a subsequent acknowledgment of an agent's authority after the agent has acted without having the initial authority.

However, in any circumstance where communication with the principal is possible, should an extraordinary occurrence take place, the agent should get further authority before taking any action and should endeavor not to take any steps without first having authority. In the case of special agents, authority is limited to the initial instructions received and is not continuous.

# 6.5    Termination of the Agency Relationship

An agency relationship can be terminated on various grounds but mainly (i) when the agent's authority is ended by an act of one of the parties, (ii) by operation of law or (iii) upon the occurrence of certain events.

An agency relationship can also be terminated upon the mutual consent and agreement of the principal and agent.

### 6.5.1    Revocation of authority by the principal

Because the principal/agent relationship is consensual in nature, the principal cannot be forced to employ an agent he does not want. The agent's authority can be revoked in any manner, regardless of the agreed method of termination. In tramp agency, the principal can immediately revoke an agent's authority agent when an agent has breached a duty of agency. In that instance, the principal is free to appoint a substitute agent.

### 6.5.2    Notification to revoke agent's authority

In general, unless otherwise agreed, the agent's authority will not end during an ongoing event or situation unless he receives notification of the principal's revocation of authority. Any word or act by the principal that indicates to the agent the principal's desire to revoke this authority is sufficient. If, however, revocation is in violation of the original agreement, the principal can be held liable for breach of contract.

### 6.5.3    Renunciation of authority by the agent

The agent also has the power to renounce the authority received from the principal. To terminate the authority, the agent must refuse to act, or notify the principal that he will not act in accordance with the instructions and authority. Renunciation of authority is effective when the principal knows of it, either in writing or by word or action of the agent. The power of renunciation is held by the agent in the same manner as revocation power is held by the principal. However, termination or renunciation of authority may leave one of the parties open to a breach of contract claim. Nevertheless, in some rare cases, it may be preferable to incur a lawsuit or settle a claim rather than continue in a relationship that one or other of the parties does not want.

### 6.5.4 Termination of the agency relationship by operation of law

Regardless of the principal's and/or agent's intention to continue their relationship, it can still be terminated by an event that makes the relationship impossible to continue. For example, a new law may suddenly render the activities contemplated by the agency relationship unlawful. In this example, the agency relationship may no longer be viable by operation of the new law.

Another example would be where the agent is not practicing under license or the principal is prohibited legally from conducting business in a particular port or jurisdiction. In these circumstances, the agency relationship cannot continue because application of local law makes the agency relationship impossible to maintain.

### 6.5.5 Termination of agent's authority due to change in circumstances

Under this category of termination, the subject matter for which the authority was originally granted is lost or destroyed. The bankruptcy of either the principal or the agent may fall into this category, as does the situation where the principal's interest in the subject matter has been extinguished. Extinguishing of the principal's interest in the subject matter would be the sale of the ship or cancellation of a time charter with the vessel owner.

### 6.5.6 Termination of agency due to war or government boycott

The outbreak of war or prohibition of commercial relations between countries of the agent and principal may be sufficient to automatically terminate the agent's authority. War or a breach in diplomatic relations between two nations will terminate the agent's authority where it would be illegal for the agent to act. The same situation exists where one nation prohibits their citizens and corporations from conducting commercial or personal business with citizens or companies of another nation.

### 6.5.7 Termination of authority by death or loss of the capacity of the agent or principal

Death of either party may be sufficient to terminate the agreement where the decedent was critical to the performance of the agency contract. Insanity of a key individual may also be sufficient to terminate the agent's authority if either the principal or agent is found to be incapable of performing their respective duties. Death or loss of capacity is usually not a sufficient basis for termination where the parties are corporations and do not act through a single, key individual.

# Chapter 7
## The Ship's Agent, Principals and Third Parties

The tramp ship agent is a special agent with limited authority to act upon specific instructions on a specific vessel and charter. The agent should take all precautions to ensure that (i) he is acting within the express authority granted to him and (ii) he does not exceed that authority. This general rule should be considered even in extraordinary situations, where the absence of immediate communication to obtain additional authority results in the agent taking preventive actions to protect the principal's interests, and with the expectation that the principal will ratify the agent's action after having learned of the agent's efforts. When the agent acts on behalf of the principal, the agent should make it clear to all third parties that he acts for a principal and that any costs or obligations are those of the agent's principal, not the agent himself.

In general, whoever concludes and signs a contract can bind himself or his company to the performance of that contract. However, if an agent stipulates to the third party with whom he is contracting that the agent is in fact bringing together the third party with a specific principal, the agent will only bind his principal and the agent will not be responsible for performance of the underlying agreement.

The phrase 'as agents only' has been used, traditionally, by agents to afford a level of protection from direct liability when dealing with suppliers, charterers, port authorities and other third parties. Use of this phrase will not be sufficient in all cases and agents should not rely unduly on the phrase's supposed protection.

Most legal treatises on agency classify agency relationships as either the disclosed principal, the partially-disclosed principal or the undisclosed principal.

## 7.1    The Disclosed Principal

The disclosed principal situation arises when, at the time of the agent's transaction with a third party, the third party is aware or has received notice of the identity of the principal the agent is acting for. A third party can receive notice of the principal's identity in several ways. As long as the third party is fully aware of the principal's identity, the principal and agent's relationship is that of the disclosed principal.

Where the principal is disclosed, the principal is the party bound to and responsible for performance of any contract concluded on the principal's behalf by an authorized agent.

## 7.2    The Partly-Disclosed Principal

The partly-disclosed principal is, in fact, undisclosed at the time of the transaction. The third party is aware of the existence of an agency relationship, but does not know the principal's precise identity. In most such cases, the partly-disclosed principal and the agent may both be liable for performance of the contract, unless it was agreed upon between the third party and the principal that the agent was acting within authority and should not be held to performance of the underlying contract. An example of a partly-disclosed principal would be a shipper or ship owner considering a charter under liner terms, where the agent has been asked to obtain stevedore costs. The principal may not want his identity to be revealed to prevent the stevedore from possibly informing a competitor. The agent's option may be to notify the stevedore, or any other vendor, that he is working on behalf of a principal that does not wish to be identified at that moment. The identity of the principal should, however, be disclosed at the earliest commercial opportunity.

## 7.3    The Undisclosed Principal

The undisclosed principal situation arises where the existence of the principal is not known or disclosed to the third party at the time of the transaction. The undisclosed principal is not bound by an agreement concluded by the agent. When an agent signs a document without disclosing that the agent is acting for a principal, the agent becomes bound to the third party for performance under the contract. The undisclosed principal cannot be brought into court by the third party for non-performance of the underlying contract.

> To summarize, an agent would be advised to disclose both that he is an agent and the identity of the principal for whom he acts. This type of disclosure will likely insulate the agent from direct liability to third parties on contracts concluded by the agent on behalf of a principal. While disclosure of the principal's precise identity may not always be possible, for example when various confidentiality stipulations may apply, the agent should still disclose the agent/principal relationship and also ensure that the principal eventually notifies the third party that the agent has been acting on behalf of the principal. Reliance solely on

the phrase 'as agent only', therefore, may not be sufficient to insulate the agent from liability to third parties.

Because of the international nature of shipping and agency, the laws of agency differ from country to country. In some countries, the agent is held liable for the principal's debts to all government authorities as well as to local vendors and suppliers. In this book, we will address third party rights as against the agent and the principal under US and UK Law as we understand them to be at this time. However, this is not intended to be an exhaustive treatment of the subject and the reader is encouraged to research the particular laws governing the jurisdictions in which they operate, or to obtain legal advice.

## 7.4 Third Party Rights Against Agent and Principal in the United Kingdom

A third party can bring a suit for damages against the agent or the principal, but not both. If the third party knows the identity of the principal, any dispute will normally be resolved between those parties. If legal proceedings are commenced, the third party would be required to prove that the principal had employed the agent for the purposes of joining himself with the third party in the transaction. But, in most cases where the principal is undisclosed, the third party will take legal action against the agent for two reasons. First, since it was the agent dealing directly with the third party, all legal documentation contains the agent's signature binding them to the contract. Second, the agent, in most cases, is domiciled in the port while the principal is unlikely to be, nor is the principal likely to be a citizen of the nation where the agent and third party entered into the transaction.

## 7.5 Third Party Rights Against Agent and Principal in the United States

In the United States, the initial threshold for commencing legal proceedings may be a bit lower than other jurisdictions. In many US jurisdictions, filing a broadly drafted pleading, payment of a filing fee and delivery (i.e. 'service') of the pleading to the defendant may be all that is required to force a party into court. The result may be that claimants will seek to also drag the agent into legal proceedings, with the hope that the agent will pressure the principal into resolving the claim. In some cases the third party may bring the agent into court for the limited purpose of determining the principal's identity.

> In general, when a lawsuit is started in a court in the United States, plaintiffs seek to cast a very wide net by naming every possible party involved or known to be involved as a defendant in the lawsuit. Given the high cost and business interruption arising from litigation, it is crucial for the agent to take steps, at the earliest stage of the agent/ principal relationship, to stay out of court. Assuming the agent takes all precautions in accordance with the authority and instructions given to him, ultimately there should be no ill consequences. However, even if eventually an agent is vindicated in a court room, substantial time and legal expense may have been incurred. Avoidance of litigation altogether is obviously the best course of action for the agent.

## 7.6    The Weakness of the 'As Agent' Signature

Given the variety of principals that an agent may represent, including even multiple principals on a single voyage, (See Chapter 4), it is crucial for the agent to have a full understanding of the relationships of the owners, charterers, and time charterers and whether they are disclosed, partly disclosed or undisclosed principals. Any other approach can lead to serious mistakes, expensive lawsuits and loss of clientele.

Signing correspondence, documentation or anything for that matter 'as agent only' can provide only a weak defense, depending upon the surrounding circumstances. Ideally, any correspondence issued by the agent, should be signed:

*XYZ Company as agents only for [name of the principal].*

The identified principal should be the one that has authorized the agent to act.

*IM Smart Ship Agency as agents only.*

The use of the phrase *"as agents only"* suffers from the deficiency that no principal is identified. Standing alone, the phrase could be read as implying that IM Smart Ship Agency is acting on its own behalf, or on behalf of an undisclosed principal. In either case, IM Smart Ship Agency is exposed to liability to third parties.

> It is important to emphasize that an undisclosed principal is not liable for the performance of a contract concluded by the principal's agent unless the principal signs the agreement personally.

The following signature may also present risks for the agent:

*IM Smart Ship Agency, as agents only, for SS Big Boat.*

In this example, the vessel's name is provided but the actual principal's identity is not disclosed. In this situation, has the agent bound his principal to an agreement with a third party? The answer will depend on what the agent is purchasing or arranging, and to whom the cost of the services or goods is allocated under the terms of the governing charter party. When the agent has disclosed the vessel's name and the time charterer fails to pay for the services or goods they received, the vessel may be arrested by a vendor asserting a maritime lien, even after the vessel has been redelivered to the owner and the defaulting time charterer is out of the picture. This can create considerable problems for the ship owner.

The following signature by the agent binds both the ship and the ship owner:

> IM Smart Ship Agency as agents for SS Big Boat and Big Boat Shipping Co.

Here there is no ambiguity that the agent acts on behalf of both the vessel and the vessel owner and the agent does not in any way bind himself to the performance of the underlying contract.

# 7.7    Creation of a Maritime Lien in the United States

In the United States, a maritime lien is created whenever a supplier provides 'necessaries' to a ship on the order of the ship owner or charterer. 'Necessaries' include, but are not limited to, stevedoring repairs, pilotage, towage, stores, provisions and bunkers. The ability to assert a maritime lien under US law is a very potent tool of the maritime claimant who is seeking to be paid for furnishing services or supplies to a particular vessel. In some cases, however, a supplier of necessaries may receive prior notice that the charter party contains a clause prohibiting the charterer from causing maritime liens to arise against the vessel. Where such prior notice is received, the necessaries claimant may lose his right to assert a maritime lien against the vessel. In reality, few providers of necessaries will agree to service a vessel if they are forced to waive their maritime lien.

In the event the vessel is on time charter, and the time charterer is responsible to bunker the vessel for his account and the agent orders bunkers in accordance with authority, a maritime lien arises in favor of the supplier even though the supplier contracted with the time charterer and not the ship owner. In the event of non-payment by the time charterer, the supplier may arrest the ship to enforce the supplier's maritime lien.

Given the severe consequences of a maritime lien to all parties involved in a ship's operations, the agent must be prudent to assure that his principals are properly identified to all third parties and that the circumstances in which a maritime lien may arise against his principal's vessels are minimized.

## 7.8    Ship Agent's Right to a Lien

Since 1855, ship agents in the United States had been unable to go to federal court under it's maritime jurisdiction to enforce agency contracts with ship owners and to assert maritime liens against their vessels. This somewhat anomalous rule dates back to the United States Supreme Court decision in *Minturn v Maynard*, which dismissed an agent's action on the basis that the agent's services were not maritime in nature and so could not support admiralty jurisdiction. However, in 1989, the US Supreme Court overturned *Minturn* in *Exxon Corp v Central Gulf Lines Inc*, thereby eliminating a 'per se' rule excluding agents' contracts from admiralty jurisdiction. Instead, the Court held that all contracts, if sufficiently maritime in nature, could be enforced under federal admiralty jurisdiction.

Once the agent is in federal court, however, the agent has the further burden of demonstrating that its services were 'necessaries' that give rise to a maritime lien. The determination of what constitutes a 'necessary' is made on a case by case basis, depending upon the nature of the services rendered. Another factor is whether the agent relied on the credit of the ship when it provided the agency services (as opposed to the credit of the ship owner or charterer) and whether the parties' agreement allows a lien in favor of the agent.

Rather than apply a per se rule, federal courts in the US will now make a two step review of most agency-type contract claims:

1.  Is the subject matter of the claim sufficiently maritime in nature to fall within federal maritime jurisdiction?

2.  Is the agreement between the parties a general agency agreement (for which no lien is allowed) or a special agency agreement from which a maritime lien may arise?

The overturning of *Minturn* does not mean that all agents' claims will be allowed under the federal court's maritime jurisdiction with access to maritime liens. Each claim will have to be assessed individually to determine whether both the jurisdictional and maritime lien components can be established by the agent.

Recommendations to agents:

*   Know clearly on whose behalf you are acting

*   have a clear understanding of which party (i.e. ship owner, time charterer, voyage charterer) is contractually responsible for the goods and services you order

*   make clear in all dealings with suppliers that you are acting solely as an agent and make as complete a disclosure of the principal's identity as the commercial circumstances allow

*   do not commit the agency's or your own personal credit for a principal.

A recent news article reported that a ship manager was sued by a vendor for spare parts supplied to the ship but for which no payment was made. In this case, the ship manager ordered the parts for the ship owner and the ship owner became bankrupt. Here, where the ship manager is paid a fixed management fee, he cannot assume any financial risk for the ship owner and the agent should be ever mindful of this in all its dealings with third parties.

Another recent example of third parties trying to impose liability on agents involved the commercial manager of a pool of ships. In that case, various ship owners appointed the commercial manager to find cargo, negotiate charters, pay port costs and appoint agents. The commercial manager was paid commissions or a fixed fee for these services. Later, when one of the ship owners failed to pay various port expenses, claims were filed against the commercial manager. However, the commercial manager successfully argued that it was merely an agent for the ship owners. Therefore, if one of the ship owners in the pool was having financial trouble, the commercial manager was not obligated to inform the agent of this fact. Although the port agent is appointed specifically to attend port calls, the ship owner remains responsible for settling the disbursement accounts.

# Chapter 8
## Duties and Liabilities of the Agent to the Principal

What are the actual duties that an agent owes to the principal? One British judge, quoted in 'Shipbrokers and the Law' by EJ Edwards, summarized the agent's duties as follows:

> *"A man who is employed to act for another as his agent, is bound to exercise all the skill and knowledge he has of the particular business, all the diligence, zeal and energy he is capable of, and any interest he may have himself, he is bound to exercise in the fullest extent for the sole and exclusive benefit of the person he is acting for".*

This book examines nine duties of agency. These duties, if breached by the agent, can give rise to liability and lawsuits if the principal is damaged. Moreover, a breach of these duties can cause the principal to lose trust and prejudice future support.

## 8.1    Duty to Act within the Scope of Authority

Under the legal definition of 'special agent', the tramp ship agent has limited authority. If an unusual or extraordinary event occurs, the agent is required to seek additional instructions and authority to act. Tramp agency appointments are from ship owners and charterers, who usually try to employ the same agent in a port on a repeat basis. Because of these prior dealings, the agent and principal are already familiar with each other and the agent is, therefore, knowledgeable about the principal's expectations in matters such as pre-arrival, in-port stay and post-sailing performance. The principal will also have experience in notifying the agent of any issue under a particular voyage or charter party that requires the agent's special attention.

However, in some bulk trades, the voyage charterer has the right to nominate the agent that the ship owner must then appoint. Therefore, in many instances, the agent and/or the ship owner are working with people they are not familiar with. Indeed, some of these principals might require the agent to seek authority in matters that may be taken for granted by another principal. Thus, when working with unfamiliar principals, agents must take care to obtain the necessary authority for their actions. Otherwise, the agent may be exposed to liability for having acted without authority and may be directly liable to third parties even though the agent thought he was contracting on behalf of his principal.

> A recommendation based upon experience: if the owner's instructions are clear but are subsequently altered by the charterer, through their right to do so, the agent should take no action and advise the owner immediately.

By way of example, consider the situation where, during the night, the charterer or receiver requires the vessel to load or discharge cargo at an additional berth, even though the charter party provides for only a single berth. If the agent does not contact the owner for additional authority due to the late hour and employs tugs and pilots to shift to the additional berth, the owner may choose not to ratify these actions, leaving the agent potentially liable for the tug and pilotage charges, and even mishandling/misdelivery of the cargo.

## Recommendation

> When cargo operation plans change, the agent cannot wait until the principal gets to the office. The ship cannot wait. Always get two after hours contacts and home phone numbers.

# 8.2    The Agent's Duty of Confidentiality and Loyalty

Because of the fiduciary nature of the agent relationship, the agent's duty of loyalty to keep the principal's business a secret is very important. This duty extends to the period of time prior to, during, and after completion of the agent's activities as the appointed vessel agent.

Disclosure of details of a principal's business may give a competitor an advantage over your principal in the marketplace. A ship owner's or charterer's success depends upon his charter negotiation techniques and the performance of his vessel. Vessel performance is often directly related to its further employment. The agent is a professional, similar to a lawyer, and breaking client confidence is a breach of the duty of loyalty. In tramp agency, with today's fast pace and smaller staff, many agents employ a VHF radio that allows for ship-to-shore communication during office hours. Often, when the owner sends a message to the agent for delivery to the Master, the agent reads it to the Master over the radio if the ship's onboard communications are not operational. Some agents state over the VHF the name of the vessel's operators, manager or charterer when giving instructions to the Master. This practice instantly allows a competitive agent to identify and try to secure the business support of that principal.

Some information contained in the owner's communication may concern the next orders or indicate that the negotiations are presently underway for the next employment. If another agent reveals all or part of this information, a competitor agent may contact their own principals, enabling them to take advantage of this otherwise private and confidential information.

**Recommendations**

**Do not mention a principal's name over the VHF or in public.**
**Do not discuss a principal's business with others.**
**Do not divulge a principal's confidential information to others.**

# 8.3    Duty and Liability to Contract on the Principal's Behalf

The tramp ship agent has implied authority to enter into contracts on behalf of the principal for those services that will enable the principal to conduct necessary vessel operations and to enter and move within a port. The agent's implied authority covers the employment of fundamental services such as pilotage, towage, launch hire, linemen, ship chandlers and other service companies.

In such cases, the agent must contract in the principal's name as per authority to do so. Each vendor, supplier or repair company must clearly know they are employed by the principal and not the agent. It would also be wise for the agent to reveal the name of the vessel owner or time charterer who is providing the authority to order these services.

When arranging tugs, ship supplies or repairs, the agent should contract as if they 'stand in the principal's shoes'. Therefore, the agent must contract for vessel services with reliable firms of known reputation for good service. This point is important as the agent may be held liable for employing parties not qualified or competent to adequately attend to the vessel. When contracting, the agent is doing so on behalf of the principal and should make clear to the service provider that only the principal is financially responsible for payment. Agents should not use their own funds to pay the principal's debts.

## 8.4    The Importance of Contract Signature

Chapter 7 discussed the legal ramifications and care to be taken by the agents when signing contracts or any documentation on behalf of the principal. 'As agents' may not be sufficient, and it is recommended to sign 'As agents for [named principal]'. The signature care is for the protection of both the principal and the agent, and it avoids any ambiguity as to whether the agent is contracting for his own account or on behalf of a specific party (i.e. the principal).

## 8.5    The Duty to Account for Funds Advanced by the Principal

When tramp vessels call at the agent's port, the best practice is for agents to request estimated port charges in advance from the principal. When funds are advanced to an agent by the principal, the agent has a duty to fully account for the principal's funds as soon as possible after the vessel sails. The unwritten rule is to account to the principal for all of the port disbursements as close as possible to 30 days after the vessel departs. This is, in some cases, difficult to comply with and the timely submission of disbursements has become a major concern in shipping circles. The disbursements are often the final correspondence between the agent and the principal and it is important that the agent leave a positive lasting impression and that port costs fall within the agent's estimate. If the agent's estimates are off, the principal should be notified immediately with an explanation.

The best recommendation for handling disbursements is to bear in mind that it is not your money. When funds are entrusted to a third party—such as an agent—the agent must at all times be able to account for these funds and must avoid intermingling them with those of the agent.

## 8.6    The Duty to Exercise Care, Skill and Diligence

The agent is under a duty to exercise, to the best of his ability and for the benefit of his principal, the skill and knowledge that is customary in tramp ship agency practice.

However, the agent is not required to guarantee satisfaction beyond what is normally expected of his services. A principal could still bring legal action against the agent if the agent breaches his duty of exercising utmost care and skill, resulting in a loss to the principal.

Mistakes do occur. Examples would be the mislabeling of a manifest causing customs fines at the discharge port; berthing the vessel at the wrong terminal causing labor standby costs and unnecessary tug and pilotage; or, misinformation or inaccurate correspondence causing the principal to take actions that would have been avoided with the correct information.

Failure to tender an NOR in accordance with the owner's instructions is another example of negligent behavior that might expose an agent to liability.

If any of these situations occur, the agent should anticipate receiving notice from the principal that the agents will be held liable for the loss and costs incurred. If the agent feels he is not liable, he may reject the claim, in which case the principal may or may not take legal action.

Errors, omissions and negligence, while not entirely avoidable, can be minimized. Agents should always be mindful and take steps to reduce the risk of mistakes.

## 8.7   Duty of the Agent to Perform all Duties Personally

This duty is worth mentioning as tramp agents often delegate some arrangements to others, such as leaving the agent's contracted transportation service to organize the hotel or customs and immigration documentation for seafarers who sign on or repatriate. The same situation may apply when the agent appoints a sub-agent to attend the ship at a nearby port. The principal may agree for the agent to use a sub-agent. However, the appointed agent remains responsible for the sub-agent's performance. These are the agent's primary responsibilities and he is, therefore, liable for their successful completion. Remember, if the car service or sub-agent fails to accomplish what they have been instructed to do on the agents behalf, the agent is still primarily responsible and cannot simply point a finger at the vendor or sub-agent.

## 8.8   Duty to Keep the Principal Informed

In tramp vessel agency, the principal relies on the agent to provide, once or twice daily, the updated loading and/or discharge prospects prior to the vessel's arrival, and while in port an update of the vessel's anticipated completion of cargo operations. In addition, while at the agent's port, the vessel may be fixed for the next employment to load. The laydays for the next voyage are based on the latest information provided by the agent. If the agent fails to keep the ship owner closely advised of any possible delays, the ship owner may lose this next cargo and revenues for the next employment. The same can occur if cargo discharge or loading orders are issued locally to the agent and the agent fails to advise the principal of changes in quantity or quality of cargo. Another example of notification relates to the effect of weather conditions on port operations and husbandry matters.

## 8.9 Notification of Principal Through the Agent

The principal will be deemed to have been notified of a fact:

- When the agent knows of the fact
- when the agent has reason to know of the fact
- when the agent has a duty to know of the fact
- when the agent has been given notification of a fact.

As an illustration of knowledge and notification in tramp agency, suppose a vessel must transit a river where the bridge clearance is 125 feet. The agent fails to notify the principal and the vessel cannot get under the bridge or, worse, the vessel collides with the bridge. It should be part of the normal business of the agent to be knowledgeable in such matters and he should, therefore, notify his principal as appropriate prior to the vessel's arrival into port.

> **Changes to or the existence of restrictions in the port where the agent practices are matters that the agent has both the reason and duty to know of and to pass on to the principal.**

If during cargo operations at port the agent learns that the shipper, receiver or charterer has changed the berth rotation, cargo quantity or quality, the agent should notify the principal immediately for authority. Otherwise, the principal's silence may be viewed as acquiescence to the change. The principal's failure to act, in turn, can affect the principal's contractual liability under the charter party or commodity sale. Changes often occur and the agent sometimes wrongly assumes that the principal has been notified, through the chartering channels, by the shipbrokers.

Do not assume anything.

> **Notification to the agent is seen as notification to the principal. Do not rely on others to relay information that the principal should possess. The principal is appointing the agent to protect his interests. The agent is responsible, therefore, for passing on information that can benefit or injure the principal.**

Consider the example where, upon the vessel's arrival at the pilot station, the terminal operators cancelled docking. The agent had a choice to place the ship at the outer anchorage to save the owner money or to bring the ship to the inner anchorage at a certain cost per day, with a waiting time limited to 48 hours. If the waiting time for the terminal exceeded 48 hours the ship would have had to return to the outer anchorage, which would have meant hiring tugs and pilotage. The usual action at this port is to anchor at the outer anchorage. The agent chose to anchor outside and send in the Master's NOR. In this instance, the voyage charterer was familiar with the port and had a charter party clause requiring the NOR to be tendered from the inner anchorage only. This was unusual and the agent was not aware of this NOR clause. The owner was displeased as this clause denied the owner the opportunity to tender an NOR from the inner anchorage. The charterer and owner had a dispute. The owner's position was that the agent should have called him on the telephone to allow him the choice of actions.

If there is any change of plan from the original schedule, the agent should inform the principal immediately. Let the principal decide what they want to do, no matter what time of day or night.

Another example of keeping a principal advised is when a ship is at anchor waiting for a berth to become available. The agent should send a daily message to the principal updating the situation. Even if nothing has changed, the agent should confirm that the situation remains the same and repeat the waiting conditions. Repeating information to the principal is better than telling them nothing at all.

Another recommendation is to give your opinion of what you think might happen in a given situation. A principal will always appreciate a phone call that explains a situation and in which the agent offers a helpful opinion or recommendation.

The worst thing that can be said about an agent is

*"they do not keep us closely advised of developments and prospects"*

or

*"we have not heard from the agent".*

Remember that your principal is a person not a thing. The ship operator has a boss. Always make the extra effort to keep the person who is the ship operator advised and make them look good before their boss. You will make a friend and, hopefully, a strong supporter of your agency business.

# Chapter 9
## Principal's Duties and Liability to the Agent

---

**This chapter explores the duties and liability that a principal may have to the tramp agent.**

## 9.1 The Principal's Duty to Provide an Opportunity for Work

Guaranteed employment is most unusual in tramp agency. The agency selection is a negotiable clause in all voyage charters. Time and bareboat charters always allow the charterer the agency selection. Therefore, an owner is unable to provide the agent unconditional employment.

In some instances, a ship owner may have a service contract with a tramp agent. Normally, in such contracts, there is a clause releasing the ship owner from employing the agent if one of their ships is on a time, bareboat or voyage charter, where the agency consignment is out of the owner's control. An owner may not need the agency to attend husbanding the ship when consigned to another agent. Agency employment is always made based upon necessity.

Where no need exists, the agent cannot contractually force a principal to guarantee employment. Guaranteed employment is more common in a liner trade. An agreement could be arranged between an agent and a shipper, receiver or charterer. For example, in some export trades, such as grain, coal or scrap, the supplier will nominate the agent under a sales contract with a shipper. The shipper may export on cost and freight terms, where they arrange to charter the ships. In this situation, the agent may have a written contract with the supplier or shipper where the shipper always negotiates control of the agency nomination on all voyage charters. A written contract between port agent and supplier and shipper is unusual. Any agent's continued employment is based upon performance satisfaction.

Having a guaranteed employment contract between the agent and a supplier or shipper is beneficial to the agent. The principal always has a choice of agents that are soliciting the principal's support, so an agent would have a difficult task convincing a principal to commit himself to a written contract guaranteeing the agent's employment.

## 9.2    The Principal's Duty of Good Conduct

The principal has a duty to conduct himself in a manner that does not discredit the reputation of the agent. This duty also implies there should be no physical or verbal abuse, by the principal, toward an agency employee.

If the agent learns of the principal having a bad reputation for engaging in illegal activities, the agent may terminate the contract or cease his service without a breach of these duties or contract.

> **This section has been included to advise tramp agents that an exit exists to discontinue serving a principal whose actions may bring the agent into trouble, or to end an association with a disreputable principal whose actions may tarnish their company's or an individual's reputation.**

## 9.3    The Principal's Duty to Pay Compensation

When an agent is requested by a principal to perform a task or service, it can be inferred that the principal is under a duty to pay the agent for that service. If the agent intentionally or unintentionally leads the principal to believe that the agent is acting for free, the principal is not under a duty to pay the agent for the services rendered.

If the agent performs a service without the principal's knowledge or authority, the principal has no duty to remunerate the agent. This could apply even if the agent's action benefited the principal.

If an agent agrees with a principal to perform a service where compensation is based on successful completion or the principal's satisfaction, the agent is not due payment should his actions be unsuccessful or unsatisfactory.

Whenever a ship agent is appointed to act as agent on a principal's behalf, the agent should always stipulate that they will do so for compensation. It is unusual that a tramp ship agent will be appointed to attend the agency for a ship and fail to state the agency fee and expenses within the request for advance disbursements for port costs. Compensation disputes often arise out of miscommunication or misunderstanding.

> ❗🔴 Employers of tramp agents, both ship owners and charterers, should be aware that agency is a service requiring fixed overhead in the same manner as any other business. Agents make a profit based upon the volume of ships attended annually. Time represents money, so any task that consumes time must be recovered financially.

When requested to perform a service beyond those of the usual ship attendance, the agent should inform the principal of either the possibility or a definite intention that compensation will be due to the agent.

Should a principal consider requesting an agent's services outside the parameters of normal ship agency duties, the principal should realize that he may be obligated to pay additional compensation. The best example is a ship owner asking the agent to seek out the best bunker prices available and then purchase a specific amount according to instructions. This service is the same as a bunker broker's, so the principal should expect the agent to request a compensation amount similar to that charged by a bunker broker.

## 9.4    Remedies of an Agent

An agent's right to a remedy if a principal breaches a contract will be determined by the law that governs the agent's relationship with the principal. If there is a written agreement it may spell out the governing law. If there is no written agreement or if the written agreement does not specify the governing law, then the local law where the agent is operating from will likely govern.

- The agent may cease to continue services

- an agent may also delay or prevent funds in transit to a principal, or may exercise a lien against any of the principal's goods or property that they hold. We mention this because the agent may be able to exercise the right of set-off or recoupment based on the governing law. Recoupment refers to the right of a defendant (i.e. the agent) to withhold (or set-off) something which is due because there is an equitable reason to withhold it; e.g. where the claimant (i.e. the principal) has breached its own obligations to the agent under the contract. Thus, if the agent's responsibilities after his appointment by the principal include collecting freights from 3rd parties, in consideration for which the principal pays the agent, the agent may have a right of recoupment vis-à-vis the collected freights for any amounts owed to the agent by the principal. However, as mentioned above, this is not a universally accepted principle and the agent will have to ascertain his rights under the governing law.

Although these remedies are available to a tramp agent, the cost of a legal action will usually far exceed the normal revenue paid for one tramp ship service. Agents may wish to keep this in mind when considering legal action.

# Chapter 10
## Indemnity Insurance for Agents

Charterers, shippers and ship owners all have insurance against the risks and perils of sea transportation. The ship owners have protection and indemnity insurance that covers such things as losses due to collisions with stationary objects, cargo damage, personal injury and government fines.

 **Agents can also take out insurance against risks arising out of the conduct of their business.**

The International Transport Intermediaries Club (ITIC) is a mutual insurance association. ITIC was created from the merger of the Chartered and International Shipbrokers P&I Club (CISBA) and the Transport Intermediaries Mutual Insurance Association (TIM). This merger, created a mutual club for ship agents, ship managers, shipbrokers, bunker brokers, sale and purchase brokers and other transportation intermediaries. ITIC generally provide professional indemnity insurance for companies involved in the transportation industry. The club defends ship agents and shipbrokers, as well as other intermediaries, and covers their professional liabilities. The club provides members with legal advice in addition to protection and indemnity against claims that arise during the course of the business of agency.

Examples of the risks of ship agency liability that are covered by ITIC include claims for professional negligence, customs and immigration fines, loss of documents and breach of warranty of authority.

## 10.1    Protection Coverage for Ship Agents

ITIC represents its tramp agency members in pursuing claims for outstanding disbursements against defaulting ship owners. It also recovers outstanding funds on behalf of ship agents and brokers and will pay for the defence of a member if an unjustified claim has been made.

The club handbook provides examples of this type of indemnity protection. In one case, a ship agent presented separate disbursement accounts to both the time charterer and the ship owner. Both the owner and the charterer refused to reimburse the agent for expenses that exceeded funds originally remitted by each. The club intervened and through its correspondents pressured both the time charterer and the owner to place the agent in funds to cover the outstanding disbursements.

An agent appointed to act on behalf of a ship owner at a discharge port was sued by the cargo receiver for damage to cargo discharged from the owner's ship. The ship owner was also sued. The club arranged for the appointment of lawyers on behalf of the agent to defend the agent's position. The action against the agent was dismissed on the grounds that the agent was acting as agent only, not as the carrier under the B/L.

Another example where P&I protection is useful is when agents are responsible for compliance with international and domestic security requirements for a ship's pre-arrival notices.

The following two scenarios are good examples of P&I protection for ship agents. In each case, the agent was required to send a notice of arrival to the Coast Guard 96 hours before the ship arrived. In both instances, the fax from the agent to the Coast Guard was received in an illegible condition, although it was possible to identify which agent had sent the fax. However, under the regulations, the Captain of the Port (Harbor Master) decided that a slightly or fully illegible fax did not represent a proper compliance with the regulations. In both instances, when the ship arrived at the pilot station and proceeded to the berth, the Coast Guard informed the agent that the arrival notice was inappropriate, the vessel's entry into port was rejected and berthing was forbidden. The ship returned to anchor out of port limits to wait for 96 hours.

In the first case, the cost of the towage and pilotage and the loss of time claimed against the agent was about $80,000. In the second instance, there was the loss of the vessel time, the towage and pilotage to return to the outer anchorage, plus the loss of hire because the ship lost the subsequent charter as she was unable to make the laydays cancelling date. The total of all the costs involved was hundreds of thousands of dollars. In both instances, the P&I Club covered the agent for the claim the owner placed against them. As a result, the owner in the second case was satisfied and retained the relationship with the agent that had gone back for decades.

## 10.2   When Agents are most Vulnerable to Claims

The most problematic times for claims to occur are Fridays, weekends and holidays. After-hours telephone calls from principals amending loading or discharge orders, which the agent must pass to the Master and ship owner, may sometimes not be recalled in detail by the person with whom you spoke.

Attending agents must ensure they have obtained all the after-office hours contacts and telephone numbers. As special agents, tramp ship agents require additional authority where situations arise out of the normal course of business.

When changing the duty agent that is to attend a vessel, it should be ensured that the handover notes are clear, all correspondences are contained in the file and that the incoming agent reviews all the details. In many instances, in the haste to get off for the weekend or holiday, the off duty agent may fail or omit to advise the incoming agent of all of the information concerning the vessel.

> **Mistakes do occur. The agency business is high pressure, with long unsocial hours where a day off or a complete night's sleep without interruption can be a rarity. Ensure that all telephone conversations, both at home and in the office, are logged in the ship's file. All orders issued by the receiver, shipper or charterer should be acknowledged in writing and copies passed to the owner.**

The time it takes to make the extra effort to keep proper records is less costly and less time consuming than the cost and length of a legal action.

The ITIC insurance cover can be a worthwhile expense to support the tramp agent when difficulties arise and can provide guidance when confronted with complex situations where legal advice could prevent an expensive error.

# Chapter 11
## Duties under a Time Charter or as a Voyage Charterer's Nominated Agent

## 11.1   Voyage Charterer's Nominated Agent

The agent's appointment to attend a vessel might not always be controlled by the ship owner. The right to appoint an agent may be contained in a charter party clause providing that the voyage charterer nominates the agent even though the ship owner is deemed to appoint the agent and pays the agent's fee and all port expenses. In this instance, the agent's authority comes from the ship owner, even though he owes his agency appointment to the charterer. Regardless, the agent is acting on behalf of the owner and is authorized by the owner to carry out all necessary acts normally performed by a ship agent.

There are many reasons for a voyage charterer insisting on the right to nominate the agent. The charterer likes the ability to have an agent who is familiar with the charterer's business and can protect the charterer's interests by keeping him informed of all developments prior to and during the vessel's port call. In addition, the charterer's nomination clause allows the charterer consistency in the personnel at any one port where cargo operations will be performed. This avoids unfamiliar agents coordinating vessel and cargo operations with the charterer's customers.

The charterer's right to nominate an agent is negotiated under almost all voyage charter parties. When an agent is nominated by a charterer and subsequently appointed by the owner, the agent has a dual duty to inform each party concurrently of the facts of the vessel's port call. Seldom does the owner or charterer object when the daily email is addressed to the owner with a copy sent to the charterer, keeping both parties to the voyage charter informed of all developments at the same time. Neither party is, or should be, denied information relating to port conditions, arrival schedule, docking prospects, and commencement and projection for the completion of the cargo operations. By keeping both parties informed at the same time, the agent maintains a neutral position and avoids appearing to favor one party over the other.

The agent should keep in mind that the charterers have two contracts to contend with – the contract of sale and the charter party – which may have different terms and conditions; i.e. are not 'back-to-back'. Therefore, the agent's role in keeping the parties informed is critical. For example, the ability of the vessel to remain safely afloat at the shipper's or receiver's berth is of interest to both the owner and charterer. In the event the Master rejects the berth as unsafe, prompt notice to both charterer and owner will allow both parties to make more informed decisions and minimize chances for a costly dispute over the safe-berth warranty of the charter party. Additionally, prior information relating to the upcoming intended cargo operations allows the charterer time to search for alternative loading or discharge arrangements and thereby avoid delay to the vessel.

A charterer could be a commodity trader, where the cargo is occasionally loaded on speculation, so the ultimate consignee of the cargo may be a party the charterer has never done business with before. In the tanker business it is common for the cargo to be sold several times before determining the ultimate consignee. Charterers prefer to control the nomination of the agent in these types of trades to protect their interests when dealing with unfamiliar parties. Here, too, when the agent simultaneously keeps the owner and charterer advised of the ultimate consignee's intentions (e.g. with the berth descriptions), the charterer is better protected from any possible claim of breach of a charter party warranty.

A nominated agent can also protect the owner and charterer in these situations by informing both parties if the original B/Ls will be available for presentation to the Master to obtain release of the cargo. If the original B/L will not be available at the discharge port when the vessel arrives, both the owner and charterer can enter into negotiations for indemnification of the owner for delivery of the cargo where the ultimate consignee is without proof of ownership. Prior notice, in this situation, can allow sufficient lead time to the owner and charterer, thereby avoiding a delay to the vessel and concurrently protecting the interests of both parties.

> **The nominated agent's purpose is to forewarn both the owner and the charterer of any port conditions or situations that may affect their relationship through the charter party, while at the same time endeavoring to expedite the vessel's cargo operations, freeing both parties to pursue subsequent business.**

The right to nominate and appoint the agent has become a negotiable term and, in many cases, the owner will submit to the charterer's nomination of the port agents to get the fixture concluded. When the charterer's nominated agent is appointed by the owner, the agent is the servant of the ship owner and remains under the ship owner's control. All actions the agent takes are only with the owner's authority. In some rare cases, the owner may be uncomfortable with the agent they are compelled to appoint and will appoint a protecting agent in addition to the charterer's nominated agent. When freight rates are low, the cost of incurring two agency fees and expense will likely prohibit this, even if some owners would find it preferable.

To accommodate some owners who are compelled to appoint the charterer's agents, many agents grant reduced agency fees to owners who wish to have their own agents husband the ship and protect their interests. The husbanding or protecting agent's fee usually reflects the agent's reduced work requirement as they are not involved with the cargo operation.

When attending a vessel as the charterer's nominated agent, it is expected that the agent will perform all services to the ship and the Master as if they had been chosen directly by the owner and without the obligation of the charter party. The agent should charge the normal agency fees for his work. The agency fees should not exceed what would have been charged under a direct appointment by the owner. Simply stated, the agent should not take advantage of the ship owner's obligatory appointment by demanding higher compensation for services.

Some agents occasionally misunderstand the duties under charterer's nomination, neglecting some of their necessary duties to the ship owner and looking after the charterer's interests only. Again, from experience as a tramp ship agent, nomination by the charterer under the charter party allows the agent an opportunity to meet and perform for a ship owner. The charterer's nomination under the charter party is free advertising and can be used to the maximum advantage to obtain future agency assignments from owners that the nominating agent would not normally have contact with.

Many ship owners have questioned the agent's ability to objectively protect the interests of both the charterer and the owner. The duality of attendance can be achieved by following the principle of special agency and acting as a conduit of information between the owner and the charterer in the event of a dispute. The agent must remember that he will not make the final decision in a dispute, but can only make recommendations that may resolve the dispute fairly to both parties or at least minimize delays to the ship's operation and sailing. In the proper passing of information or protests between parties in accordance with authority and instructions received, the agent should have no fear of jeopardizing this authority or showing bias to one party over another. Indeed, in tanker chartering, it is common practice for one broker to act for both the owner and the charterer, with neither the owner nor the charterer objecting.

The agent's critical role as an unbiased 'conduit of information' can also be illustrated in cases where the agent is asked to pass a Master's letter of protest to the receivers, shippers and charterers. To emphasize the impartiality of the agent, the agent should present the protest with the following preamble:

"We have been instructed by the Master and the owner to deliver to you the following Master's letter to protest QUOTE........UNQUOTE."

This type of preamble will help avoid the appearance that the agent is favoring one party over another.

When an agent is uncertain about the scope of his responsibilities in the context of dual representation, he should be guided by the fundamental principle that he is a special agent. Therefore, it would be wise for any company in ship agency to ensure that all members of the tramp agency department are fully conversant with the key principles of special agency.

# 11.2    Ship Agent's Duty Under Time Charter

Under a time charter, the vessel owner charters (i.e. leases) his vessel to a charterer (i.e. the lessee) for a period of time stated in the charter party contract. During the time charter period, the vessel owner continues to maintain the vessel, employs and pays the crew and pays for the expenses of running the vessel. The charterer obtains no property interest in the vessel but pays for bunkers, pilots, tugs and other port charges arising at the ports to which he sends the vessel. The charterer also arranges to load his own cargoes, or those of other sub-charterers to whom the charterer has sub-chartered the vessel under voyage charters he fixes as an operator.

In return for the use of the vessel during the time charter period, the time charterer pays the owner a fixed rate per day known as hire. The charterer's hire payment is usually payable in advance every fifteen days, or at some other interval stipulated in the charter party agreement. After the vessel is delivered by the ship owner to the charterer, pursuant to the time charter, the charterer assumes responsibility for the vessel's employment and has the right to instruct the Master as to the prosecution of the vessel's voyages. First and foremost, the charterer will be concerned with finding suitable cargoes for the vessel during the time charter period. Fixing suitable cargoes may be carried out in the open charter freight market or the charterer may have hired the vessel for the carriage of his own cargo to avoid fluctuations in the charter market. In a time charter, the Master has a dual function; i.e. agent for the time charterer and employee of the owner.

Items provided by the owner under a time charter include:

- Stores and provisions for the crew
- wages for the officers and crew
- insurance
- maintenance of hull and machinery in a seaworthy condition
- maintenance of Classification and cargo gear approval
- lighting on deck and in the holds

- fresh water for the crew
- use of dunnage and shifting boards on board.

The time charterer's responsibilities include:

- Payment of hire
- towage and pilotage
- port agency attendance
- payment of customs, light and canal dues
- cargo handling
- additional dunnage and shifting boards or any other cargo handling equipment
- bunkers
- port charges for all ports to which the charterer directs the vessel.

The commercial objective of a time charter is to share the duties of a carrier of goods over a period of time, with the hope that both parties will benefit from the vessel's earnings. In the sharing of those duties between owner and charterer, the Master is the employee of the owner for the navigation and management of the vessel in accordance with the charterer's needs. The Master is the agent for the time charterer on all matters relating to the cargoes arranged by the charterer.

As the operator of the vessel, the time charterer has the right to appoint the agents at both the load and discharge ports, except where the time charterer sub-lets the vessel to a voyage charter, in which case the voyage charterer will have the right to nominate their own agents. Therefore, the time charterer, acting as disponent owner, must appoint and pay all agents' fees, expenses and port charges.

As specified in most time charters, the agent is to be appointed by the time charterer and usually attends to all of the ship's matters in the port.

In some instances, the ship owner deems it necessary to appoint his own protecting or husbandry agent to attend to those duties provided by the owner under a time charter. In such a case, the owner's appointed agent should restrict his activities to the owner's matters only and take no action that would interfere with cargo operations or the activities of the time charterer or his appointed agents. Agents appointed by the time charterer should attend to the joint needs of both the owner and the time charterer and see that they are coordinated in a manner that neither party's requirements interfere with the objectives or duty of the other in the shared venture.

Some agents question whether they can act for more than one principal under a time charter agency appointment.

The agent's duties to both the time charterer and the owner will vary, depending upon two key issues:

1.  The business relationship between the time charterer and the owner and

2.  the method of allocating port disbursements between the parties.

Duty-sharing will be negatively impacted when one party accuses the other of lack of cooperation. In such a situation, the time charterer may request that its agent make a personal assessment of the vessel's appearance and performance. The owner will appoint his own agent at the port to make an assessment of whether or not the time charterer's in-port demands are in excess of normal terms.

The time charterer and the owner may be leading up to a commercial dispute, in which case the agent must be very objective and diplomatic in the presentation of his assessments. If a situation exists where the time charterer and owner are having a contentious relationship, it would be wise for the owner to appoint his own protecting agent.

However, in a normal situation, the agent can adequately attend to the duties and requirements of both the time charterer and the owner by endeavoring to coordinate each party's needs in a manner that does not adversely impact the rights of the other party. An example of this is voyage repairs. The owner has the duty to maintain the vessel in a seaworthy condition that will not affect the cargo operations of the vessel. Therefore, diligent effort by the agent is required to coordinate vendors and service attendance to the vessel, in conjunction with cargo operations, so that all vessel requirements are completed without delaying cargo operations or sailings.

The second key circumstance that may affect the agent's ability to service both the owner and the time charterer, without additional compensation, would be in the settling of disbursements. In some time charters, the time charterer will pay for husbandry expenses up to a fixed amount and then deduct this expense from the next hire payment. As outlined earlier, the time charterer will advance funds to his agent to cover a ship's port costs, cargo related expenses and bunkers. All matters relating to crew, vessel maintenance and stores are to be paid by the owner. Often, the time charterer appoints an agent, with specific instructions that for any and all costs related to servicing the owner's affairs, the agent is to solicit the owner in advance for separate authority and funds. In these cases, the time charterer specifically withholds authority from the agent to commit the charterer's money or credit for the ship owner's needs. When this occurs, the appointed agent must obtain specific authority to act on behalf of the owner. Nevertheless, the agent should be entitled to compensation from the owner through an agency fee for the services performed specifically for the ship owner.

It should be noted that a husbanding agency fee is generally less than a full consignment fee charged to the time charterer, since the amount of work, time spent and risk to the agent is different.

However, this does not condone an agent charging an owner unreasonable fees for such services. The agent's fee should reflect the amount of time and effort taken to service an owner's husbanding needs and takes into consideration that an additional fee is being earned from the time charterer.

> The agent's duty to both parties can be handled in a manner that mutually benefits them by fostering and maintaining a cooperative relationship in the venture. If a dispute does arise, the agent must bear in mind that he will not make any final decision, but will act only as a conduit between both parties, passing information to each and at all times being objective.

## 11.3   Disbursements Under Time Charter

The disbursements under a time charter can be handled in a number of ways, depending on the wishes of both the owner and the time charterer and how the charter party agreement allocates responsibility between the parties for various costs and port expenses.

### 11.3.1   Non-separation

Here, the agent does not separate the invoices covering owner's and time charterer's expenses. The bills and supports are documented in the disbursements account as would normally be done for any ship owner on a voyage charter. The agent presents the complete account to the time charterer, who will separate the owner's and charterer's accounts. The time charterer will then remit funds to the agent to cover both the time charterer's port costs and the ship owner's husbandry costs. The time charterer then seeks reimbursement directly from the ship owner or makes a deduction from future hire payments. In some charter parties the time charterer is allowed a fee for providing this service. In the 'New York Produce Exchange' form and the 'Shell Time' form, the time charterer can deduct up to 2.5% of the amount he has disbursed on the owner's behalf. In the 'Intertanktime' form, the service is 1.5%, and in the 'Linertime' it is 1%.

Usually in this case, the owner and the time charterer have a normal relationship and the agent is not allowed to invoice the ship owner separately for covering the owner's matters.

### 11.3.2   Separation of disbursements at the time charterer's request

In this situation, the time charterer instructs the agent that, for all owner's matters, the agent is to look to the owner for funds in advance and is not to use the time charterer's disbursements or credit. In such a case the agent should request, from the owner, funds in advance and obtain their authority to act on their behalf. Provided the owner appoints the agent and authorizes him to act, the agent is allowed to charge a separate agency fee to the owner in addition to the agency fee received for attending to the time charterer's matters.

Alternatively, under this category, the charterer may agree to place the agent in funds to cover all of the owner's expenses, but to separate the account. In this instance, the agent is not usually appointed by the ship owner and so is not permitted by the time charterer to charge an additional agency fee for attending to the owner's husbandry matters.

### 11.3.3    Separation of accounts at owner's request

This is similar to separation at the time charterer's request in that the owner appoints the agent directly and agrees to accept the agent's fee to service the owner's matters separately, in addition to attendance to the time charterer's matters.


# 11.4    Attendance of Delivery and Redelivery

As time charters are concerned with the payment of hire by the charterer over a specified period of time, the commencement and cessation of the time charter period is of key importance to both parties. For example, the charterer's obligation to pay hire generally begins and ends after 'delivery' of the vessel to the charterer and 're-delivery' of the vessel back to the ship owner. The agent's role in determining when delivery and re-delivery has taken place and in determining when the vessel is on-hire or off-hire is, therefore, of paramount importance.

At the time delivery, the vessel will usually go on-hire at the pilot station while taking on the inward pilot. In such a case, the owner and time charterer will request the agent to obtain from the pilot the exact time he and the Master agree that boarding took place. At the vessel's arrival at anchorage or berth, the 'on hire survey' will take place. This involves an independent surveyor, appointed by the agent, who surveys the quantity of bunkers on board, assesses the condition of the vessel - particularly the cargo areas - for any damage and, finally, inspects the holds and/or tanks to ascertain that they are fit to carry the intended cargoes.

The bunkers on board the vessel at the time of delivery at the pilot station are also calculated jointly by the surveyor and the Master. The on-hire delivery certificate will confirm that the on hire survey was completed and will state the time, place and date of the survey, and the quantity of bunkers on board at the time of delivery. The certificate is signed by the Master, surveyor, chief engineer and agent as witness.

Re-delivery of the vessel back to the ship owner at the conclusion of the time charter period is a similar process in that it determines the quantity of bunkers on board the vessel and determines completion of the time charterer's and owner's liability under the charter. Since the time charterer is responsible for providing bunkers to the vessel during the time charter period, re-delivery bunkers are usually the property of the time charterer for accounting purposes,

In both instances the agent is the coordinator of the surveyors and should ensure timeliness of the delivery and re-delivery facts.

The agent also plays an important role in cases where the charterer declares the vessel 'off-hire' because of some deficiency in the vessel's performance. When a vessel is declared off-hire, the charterer suspends the payment of hire to the ship owner on the basis that the charterer does not have complete use of the vessel. For example, if the vessel has an engine breakdown and must put into a lay berth for repairs, the agent will coordinate the vessel's shifting into lay berth and is the party who will determine when the vessel was diverted off the service of the time charterer; i.e. when it went off-hire. The agent will also determine at what stage of the completion of repairs the vessel returned to the service of the time charterer; i.e. when the vessel went back on-hire. The agent will also often be involved in coordinating a survey to determine the quantity of bunkers on board at the time the vessel went off-hire and the return to hire period.

> The agent is to attend to the time charterer's duties covering both cargo matters and vessel operations. At the same time, he covers the services needed by the owner of the vessel to keep the vessel maintained in good condition, and performs any services that arise from each party's joint duties under the charter party.
>
> There is no reason why the agent cannot service the interests of both so long as each is in agreement and is aware that the agent is attending to the interests of each other. Provided the agent remains within the boundaries of special agency and acts objectively, only acting as a conduit during disputes, the agent should not prejudice his position of acting for both principals.

# Chapter 12
## How to Select a Tramp Ship Agent

An owner will often have a directory of agents they have worked with over the years and, if there are no negative comments in the file, they will use that agent again. When faced with the situation of having to choose an agent for the first time, the principal should request the following information from several agents:

- A brief history of the firm, including whether it is privately held, a joint venture or a subsidiary of a larger organization

- list of senior managers and their after office hours contact details

- directory of port offices and after office hours contact details for the operations staff

- brief list of principals

- whether they are involved in other maritime related services

- port and berth restrictions and a detailed breakdown of port costs for one of the ships being considered for a voyage into that port.

> **A survey of several agents will usually find at least three agents that provide quick and informative responses. One or two may make the extra effort to telephone the principal to follow up and discuss the enquiry. An enquiry of this type should help to determine which agent will be best suited to take care of your needs.**

## 12.1 The Agent is a Reflection of the Party who Nominates or Appoints

When nominating or appointing an agent, a principal is placing before those he does business with an organization he believes will act and perform to the same standards as he does. Therefore, the principal's customers and those with whom he contracts will have the natural tendency to accept the principal's preferred agent as an organization whose business methods and service attitude are quite similar to those of the principal. This is a reasonable position as the agent is authorized to act in accordance with the principal's wishes or, as stated earlier, the agent stands in the shoes of the principal. Therefore, the nominating or appointing party is placing their reputation on the line each time they select a port agent. The port agent will interface with all parties involved in any one voyage, such as shippers, charterers, ship owner, shipboard personnel, government agencies and vendors or service firms, so their actions and professionalism are open to be judged by all.

Great care should be exercised when selecting a tramp agent, especially considering the possible liabilities carried by a principal to a third or contracted party for the agent's actions.

## 12.2    Financial Strength

An insolvent agent could create a liability for either time charterers or voyage charterers and, therefore, the financial strength of an agent is of paramount importance. If a nominated or appointed agency enters bankruptcy, the reflection and implication upon the nominating or appointing party can be quite severe, particularly for an owner whose vessel is on time charter. If the time charterer's agent goes bankrupt and the time charterer does not accept the loss and pay his port costs again, it could be the owner's vessel that is arrested by local vendors.

No ship agency enters insolvency overnight. The process has tell-tale signs, some more obvious than others: staff lay-offs, a decrease in service quality due to insufficient staffing and low morale, delayed payments of port charges and the departure of key personnel. Rumors about an agent's financial status may not be reliable and should be verified by asking the agent to prove their solvency with documentation from their bankers. A principal can also contact the tug and pilot firms to verify the agent's credit reputation. If there is any concern, it is probably best for the principal to select another agent until the financial status of the agent in question is verified.

## 12.3    The Reporting of Voyage Accounting

The rendering of an account of a principal's advanced funds to cover port charges should be completed by the tramp agent within 30 to 40 days after the ship sails from port. Unfortunately, not all vendors and government agencies are prompt about submitting their invoices. It should not be necessary to delay forwarding the principal the entire accounting because one or two invoices are missing. This particular issue is one of the most repeated complaints against tramp agents. Lengthy delays rendering disbursement accounts may indicate more than just clerical backlog and could even point to misuse of a principal's funds by an agent using them to cover company expenses.

Quite often, an owner must deal with an agent he is unfamiliar with. If the owner is cautious, he may put a protective agent in advance funds to disburse to the nominated agent. He may also consider advancing the funds to his local P&I Club representative to disburse to the unfamiliar agent or port vendors. P&I Clubs are seldom used in such a manner, but at times it is worth inquiring or requesting this assistance.

> An owner committed to the charterer's right to nominate the agent could consider rejection of an agent they fear could misuse funds or who has a poor reputation. The owner can request the charterer to nominate another agent or accept the owner's preferred agent. If forced to use a nominated agent of disrepute, the charterer should be asked to indemnify the owner for the acts of the charterer's chosen agent.

## 12.4   Communication and Cargo Documentation

In addition to financial status, the way an agency handles communications and cargo documentation is of major importance. An agent should not have to be told that daily communication with principals (owners or charterers) is fundamental. Communicating is one of the main reasons for employing the agent. Another reason is the timeliness and accuracy of the cargo and voyage documents, such as the statement of facts, port logs, mates' receipts, bills of lading, cargo manifests, notice of readiness and surveyor's reports.

When considering an unfamiliar agent, the principal should telephone them and request details of their communication procedures and how long they generally take to prepare and send cargo and voyage documents. The relevant documents should be dispatched by the agent within 24 hours after the ship sails.

Alternatively, a principal may contact the agent with specific instructions detailing the frequency of and the facts required in each report.

In view of the various demurrage claim time-bar clauses incorporated into voyage charters, receipt of cargo and voyage documents in a timely manner is crucial. When working with an unfamiliar agent, it might be wise for a principal to instruct the agent to dispatch documents electronically and send the originals by one of the many worldwide air courier services. When proceeding this way, care should be taken to instruct the agent to advise the principal of the name of the courier company, the date the documents were dispatched and the airway bill number.

## 12.5    Company and Agency Staff Experience

Not all agency companies have the expertise to handle different types of tramp vessels and their associated commodities. Some agents may only have liner ship agency as their main area of business and are, therefore, inexperienced with charter parties or handling of tankers, dry bulkers, auto carriers or specialized chemical tankers. Inexperienced staff can cause difficulties for a shipmaster, owner or charterer, so it is crucial to know beforehand whether the particular agency has the in-house knowledge to handle the particular vessel and/or cargo.

One way for a principal to ascertain this information is to contact the agent directly and ask outright what experience the staff has and request references from other clients. A principal could also request a familiar nearby agent to act as the head or appointed agent, allowing that agent to appoint a sub-agent at the unfamiliar port. The familiar agent should be instructed to supervise and guide the sub-agent's actions.

## 12.6    Worldwide Ship Agency Networks

There are various ship agency companies that maintain offices in hundreds of ports around the world and employ thousands of people. Some of these companies are privately held and some are publicly traded firms. There are also networks and associations comprising many ship agencies, such as the Association of Ship Brokers and Agents (USA) Inc and the Multiport Ship Agencies Network. The Multiport Ship Agencies Network is an association of independent members made up of port agents in nearly every port in the world. All of the firms are very well known and are accessible through the internet.

A good ship agency is judged one ship at a time. An organization with a vast global network of port offices does not necessarily guarantee that all ports will offer the same service consistency. An agent dedicated to serving in only one port or country may very well be as good as or better than the agent with a global enterprise behind him. Neither the size of the company nor the number of staff employed determine how well the agency will perform. It all depends upon the people.

> **The agent provides the primary access to the key decision makers in the port, such as government authorities, port and terminal managers, vendors and ship suppliers.**
>
> **They have knowledge and experience in local and national regulations to guide the principal's activities legally and in a cost effective manner. This may also include knowledge of unique or unwritten rules or customs of the port, local traditions or the protocol of courtesies within the local ethnic, tribal and government authorities.**

The agent provides the principal's credit worthiness with public and private terminals, government agencies and service providers. At any given time, changes may occur that impact the budget for port costs advanced to the agent. The agent's credit locally allows the principal to continue port operations via the agent's promises to vendors and service providers until the principal can remit more funds.

Simply stated, the agent is the 'can do, go to' guy when the principal needs help to solve a problem. These qualities cannot be measured by a website appearance. The principal that has a good relationship with an agent will recognize and respect the agent's intangible qualities and skills.

# Chapter 13
## Maintenance of the Agent/ Principal Relationship

A tramp agent requires a specific number of vessel appointments per year to cover operating costs and produce a profit. Therefore, as a business concern dependent upon numerical volume, the agent must secure as many principals as possible who will provide long-term repeated appointments.

The long-term principal to agent relationship has two characteristics: personal and corporate. The personal relationship is between the employee within a principal's firm who controls agency selection and an employee or employees working within the agency firm. The corporate relationship refers to the confidence that the management of the principal's firm has in the management of the agency firm, gained through an understanding of their philosophy on retention of knowledgeable personnel, their business practices and their history of responsiveness to the needs of the principal.

## 13.1 The Personal Relationship and Corporate Relationship

Within the ship owner's or charterer's organization, the person conducting operations usually controls the agency selection. This person has direct contact with the agent and is, therefore, in a position to judge one agent's skill against another's. The principal's employee develops confidence in an agent and his responsiveness to questions.

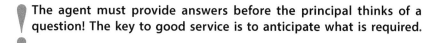

**The agent must provide answers before the principal thinks of a question! The key to good service is to anticipate what is required.**

The personal relationship is usually solidified by regular telephone contact, which is often easier than writing an email. It is easier to form an impression of another person via regular telephone contact and a verbal communication can indicate whether the agent is generally organized, knowledgeable, courteous and reliable in a crisis.

Another aspect of the personal relationship is the reliance of the principal's employee upon the agent's employee. This can cause a dilemma if the favored agency staff member leaves the agency firm. Quite often, if an agency operations person who has considerable direct contact with principals joins another agency firm, the principal may change agents to maintain the relationship. In a defence against this, the development of the corporate relationship is extremely important.

In the same manner, a change of operations personnel within the principal's firm can cause the agent to lose support because the new staff member may have his own preference for agents.

The corporate relationship is often historical in nature, particularly where an agent's and principal's operations staff have developed a friendship and subsequently been promoted within their respective firms while maintaining their association. The management of the principal and the agent will use the long-term association, instructing the principal's personnel to continue employing the agent and informing the agency personnel of the importance of a specific principal. This is in spite of changes that may take place at the operational level within the agent's business. If the agent's service remains consistently good and the principal's management feel assured they have direct access to the agency management who will endeavor to provide the best personnel to service the principal, there should be no problem with business retention. At the same time, the principal should feel confident if they need to criticize the agent's service, to the agency management, that he will obtain a prompt response and remedy.

To develop a strong personal and corporate relationship, the agent must make the effort to visit the principal, or at least communicate personally, on a regular basis. The frequency of visits by the agent would depend upon the financial gain provided by the principal's support.

> **The principal will appreciate that an agent went to the effort and expense to travel to visit them. It demonstrates interest in the principal's business. People do business with people that they like. If you don't make the effort to visit your customers, you are out of sight, out of mind and will eventually be just out.**

For every agency appointment, it is recommended that the agent telephones the person who sent the appointment notice while the ship is still in port to say all is okay with the ship and to ask if they have any concerns. Ask if there is anything else that you can do. If you get the voice mail, leave a message. Ask the question and say that you're making a courtesy call to follow up your service. This is all part of making the extra effort to show interest.

In addition to personal visits, the agent should update any cost changes or port restriction changes that may affect the principal's interests. This effort indicates that the agent is concerned for and functions on behalf of the principal even though the principal has no ship in port.

If an agent fails to develop and maintain personal and corporate relationships, personnel changes within the agent's or principal's firms can cause loss of the principal's ongoing support.

> **It is less costly to maintain an existing customer than it is to develop a new customer.**

## 13.2    The Trade Relationship

It is common for commodity traders, as a courtesy to their customers receiving the cargo and to shippers selling the cargo, to allow selection of the nominated agents to the ship operator in the charter party. This is commonly known as shipper's or receiver's agent. It will guarantee a port agent regular business. The agent can charge a full agency fee and may even expand services to the shippers or receivers, such as surveying, tallyman and other logistics.

Another method of maintenance of a principal relationship is to develop a relationship within the commodity trade that the principal serves. Agents must see the big picture of the commodity trades served from their port and see themselves as a participant within a trade rather than just a servant to the ship operator or the charterer.

A port agency's fee comes from the commodity trade, regardless of who recommends or selects and pays the agent. To protect their market position, the agent must be known by all participants and create a positive relationship with those parties, even though the agent's scope is limited to the port operations as the ship operator's or the charterer's nominated agent. The reason for taking this approach is to prevent the loss of ship volume and revenue source in the event that the principal with whom the agent is associated loses the contract or is replaced by another owner, charterer or trader in the same commodity trade. Agents should create the image that they are the port agents for the commodity trade and be known by all those involved in the trade as the agent who is responsive, knowledgeable and concerned for a smooth port operation for everyone involved. This requires a sensitive approach to the business because of the potential risk of being perceived as having conflicts of interest.

The way to develop trade relationships is to meet the participants and gain an understanding of their aspects of the business. It will be beneficial for the agent to personally meet all parties involved in the movement of a commodity through his port. For example, he should get to know the terminal staff, trucking or rail managers, forwarders, surveyors, etc. Anyone who is associated with the commodity should be an acquaintance of the agent. Situations always eventually change. The shipper, receiver or terminal may some day influence the choice of agents and your company wants to be foremost on everyone's mind as the most knowledgeable. Try to think of ways of being helpful, seek solutions and create value added services to offer all the participants within the trade. Trade shows and conferences with a focus on a commodity provide a good venue to meet all the players in that trade. After meeting people at a trade show, it is important to follow up with written communication and/ or visits. The alternative to the trade show is to personally visit as many people as possible in your country who are involved in the commodity you are depending upon.

> **It is important that agents maintain a strong relationship with each of their principals. They should expand from those associations to see the big picture of the commodity trade and develop into the recognized agent for the whole trade, with all participants supportive of the agent's continuation regardless of any changes that may take place.**

# Chapter 14
## Charterer's Liability for Actions of a Nominated Agent

---

This chapter considers whether a charterer can be held liable for the acts of a nominated agent, even though the agent is actually employed and compensated by the ship owner.

## 14.1 The Charter Party Agency Clause

As discussed elsewhere, it is customary in certain trades to grant to the charterer the right to 'nominate' or select a particular agent at loading and discharge ports. This privilege is normally set out in a clause contained in the charter party known as the agency clause.

The actual wording of the agency clause will vary depending upon the printed form or trade. An example would be the 'GENVOY' form of charter party, which contains the following clause:

> "Agency
>
> At the port(s) of loading and the port(s) of discharge, Charterers are to have the privilege of appointing vessel's agents, Owners paying customary fees".

Other charter party clauses, though worded differently, encompass the same concept as the GENVOY form; i.e. expressly granting to the charterer the right to nominate the port agent whose services will be paid for by the ship owner.

The selection of a port agent by the charterer pursuant to an agency clause is often referred to as a 'nomination.' However, as in the case of the GENVOY charter form, the term 'appointment' may also be used interchangeably. The key point to remember is that the nomination/appointment of an agent pursuant to an agency clause does not alter the fact that the ship owner is the agent's principal and the party responsible for paying the agent.

## 14.2    The Incentive for a Voyage Charterer to Nominate the Port Agent

In most of the major and minor bulk trades, the charterer will try to secure the right to select port agents, even though the agents are formally engaged and compensated by the ship owner. Historically, the ship owner was free to choose his own agent at the load and discharge ports, and some charter party forms continue to preserve this right.

In a weak freight market, the ship owner will generally agree to a charterer's agency clause in the charter party rather than lose the fixture. Nevertheless, even in a strong owner's market, the charterer's agency clause has become customary in many bulk and tanker trades. Early on in fixture negotiations, owners often ask for owners' agents, although it is not usually a source of serious disagreement.

In many cases, the charterer will be an ongoing concern within a given commodity trade, familiar with the ports, terminals, shippers, receivers and peculiarities of the trade. The charterer's ability to control the agency selection allows for a continuity of service in the form of personnel familiar with particular cargoes and local port operations. Such continuity can minimize delays caused by inexperienced ship's staff. Furthermore, the agent nominated by the charterer will also likely be attentive to the charterer's interests and assure compliance with the terms of the charter party and other obligations of the charterer to the shipper or receiver. The agent must not forget, however, that his principal is still the ship owner, not the charterer making the initial nomination.

Because the charterer is often also a commodity trader, the charterer must also endeavor to coordinate the charter party terms and conditions with those of the contract for the sale or purchase of the cargo. By selecting a port agent knowledgeable in a specialized trade, the charterer is providing experience and consistency of service to minimize performance issues.

Although it may seem that the charterer is deriving free port agent services with the right to nominate the agent, in fact port costs and agency fees are included within the freight rate. Consequently, the charterer actually does pay for these cost and fees.

## 14.3    The Charterer must Make a Reasonable Appointment

Does the voyage charterer have any duty to the ship owner, or to third parties, when he selects a port agent pursuant to a charter party agency clause? In considering this question, the concept of reasonableness has to be examined; i.e. was a particular nomination reasonable under the prevailing circumstances and information then known to the charterer? A reasonable nomination measures the appropriateness of a particular action against the action any other reasonable person (or charterer) would have taken under similar circumstances within the custom or practice of a specific trade.

These principles are illustrated in a 1985 New York arbitration award of the Society of Maritime Arbitrators, *The S/T ATHENA*, SMA No. 2178 (1985). In that case, a ship owner's demurrage claim was found to be time-barred pursuant to a 'Demurrage Claim Clause' in the charter party. The ship owner sought to excuse the late submission of the claim by blaming the port agent for failing to provide all the necessary supporting documentation in sufficient time to allow the ship owner to prepare the demurrage claim within the time bar period. The ship owner argued that, since the agent had been selected and appointed by the charterers, the charterers should bear responsibility for the agent's delay, not the ship owner.

The arbitration panel rejected the ship owner's argument and refused to find any negligence in the charterers' selection of the port agent. As the panel noted, *"appointment of an agent does not render the appointer responsible for the acts of the agent so long as the appointment is reasonable."*

The lesson that can be derived here is that the mere nomination of an agent pursuant to a clause of the charter party will not automatically make the party nominating the agent liable for the actions of that agent.

The duties of an agent with respect to port clearance and their impact on the rights of a ship owner and charterer, were examined in another more recent New York arbitration, *The NOVA CALEDONIA*, SMA No. 4066 (2010). In that case, the charterer appointed the port agent on behalf of the ship owner as permitted by the charter party. The Master then requested that the agent assist him in filing the required 96 hours notice of arrival with the US Coast Guard. However, incorrect documents were submitted and the vessel's entry was denied for an additional 96 hours, causing the ship owner to miss the cancellation dates of the charter party. Consequently, the charterer cancelled the charter party on the basis that the vessel was not ready or able to load within the time required by the contract.

The ship owner rejected the charterer's position and commenced arbitration to recover damages for wrongful cancellation. The ship owner asserted that the charterer should bear responsibility for the agent's failure to clear the vessel, because the charterer nominated the agent. The arbitration panel rejected this argument, finding that although the agent was 'nominated' by the charterer, the agent was employed and compensated by the ship owner. Therefore, the agent was the ship owner's agent for purposes of assigning responsibility for the agent's actions.

## **14.4** Liability for the Insolvency of the Agent

Which party bears responsibility for losses arising out of the insolvency of an agent nominated by the charterer pursuant to an agency clause? For example, a ship owner may advance funds to the nominated agent to pay for port costs and local vendors. What happens if the agent becomes bankrupt and the funds advanced by the ship owner are wiped out? The ship owner in these cases will often be forced to pay the third parties directly in order to avoid arrest of the vessel; effectively paying for the same port costs twice. Should the charterer bear any responsibility for having nominated an agent that was, ultimately, financially unsound?

Here, again, the doctrine of reasonable appointment will come into play in determining whether the charterer bears any responsibility for losses caused by the insolvent agent. A key factor will be whether the charterer had actual or constructive knowledge that the agent was insolvent (or nearly insolvent) at the time of the initial nomination. Constructive knowledge consists of indirect information that should have alerted the charterer to the poor financial condition of the agent selected under the agency clause.

In the absence of actual or constructive knowledge of the agent's insolvency at the time of the nomination/appointment, the charterer will have no independent duty to assure the continued solvency of the selected agent. In other words, assuming the initial nomination was reasonable, the charterer is not a guarantor of the agent's future solvency.

## **14.5** Charterer's Liability Through the Implied Agency Doctrine

An agent can bind the parties to a charter party agreement, including the charterer, through the legal doctrine of implied agency. An agency may be implied based on the parties' conduct and the totality of the surrounding circumstances, even if the usual formalities (i.e. a written agreement) are absent. Once an implied agency is found, a principal is bound by the agent's acts even if no formal agency relationship exists.

Courts, when asked to determine whether an agency relationship exists, are not bound by the name or title the parties give to their relationship. A court may find that an agency relationship exists even when the parties deny that they intended to establish such a relationship. A good statement of this principle can be found in *Interocean Shipping Company v National Shipping and Trading Corporation*, 1975 AMC 1283, 1297 (2d Cir. 1975), where the court had to decide whether a particular broker/agent had authority to bind various parties. As the court noted, the actual intent of the parties was not the controlling factor: *"Agency is a legal concept which depends on the manifest conduct of the parties, not on their intentions or beliefs as to what they have done."*

A charterer should, therefore, be alert to the possibility that a nominated agent, although formally employed and paid by the ship owner, may also bind the charterer under the implied agency doctrine. No magic formula is necessary to give rise to an implied agency. A party's words and conduct in the context of the surrounding circumstances may be sufficient.

## 14.6 Charterer's Liability in Cases Where the Nominated Agent is Acting for a Limited Purpose

On occasion, the agent nominated by the charterer, although employed and compensated by the ship owner, may act for a limited or special purpose at the request of the charterer. In these cases, courts have had to clear up confusion concerning whether the agent was acting for the charterer or the ship owner. In *Tarstar Shipping Company v Century Shipline Ltd,* 1979 AMC 1096 (2nd Cir. 1979), the voyage charterer authorized its nominated agent to collect sub-freights from various consignees and then to pay a portion of these sub-freights to the disponent owner. However, the ship owner had also asserted its own lien on these same sub-freights for non-payment of hire by the disponent owner. Despite the ship owner's lien, the agent paid the collected sub-freights to the disponent owner who, in turn, became insolvent and failed to pay the ship owner its hire. The ship owner then commenced legal proceedings against the ship agent and other parties seeking to collect the unpaid hire from them.

In finding in favor of the ship owner, the court concluded that the agent was acting here as a 'payment agent' for the sub-charterer and that the sub-freights should not have been paid in light of the ship owner's notice of lien. Consequently, the sub-charterer was found liable to pay the ship owner for the losses caused by the agent's wrongful actions.

## 14.7 The Ship Owner's Ratification of the Charterer's Agency Nomination

Where the ship owner accepts the charterer's selection of a particular agent, the owner may be deemed to have ratified the agency selection and may subsequently be barred from claiming that the charterer's nomination was unreasonable.

Because tramp ship agency is essentially a form of special agency, a prudent ship owner will take protective measures by expressly limiting the port agent's authority to specific matters. The agent must then be careful to adhere to these specific instructions and avoid circumstances where the charterer seeks to have the agent take steps that are outside the scope of the special instructions provided by the ship owner.

A prudent ship owner will instruct the agent to seek specific owner's authorization for any actions relating to a vessel's movement and cargo operations. Similar instructions can be given to the agent concerning the disbursement of funds advanced by the ship owner. Finally, the ship owner should also notify the charterer of the limitations imposed on the nominated agent's authority.

Of course, if a ship owner objects to the charterer's nomination they can always appoint a protecting agent. While this results in the ship owner having to pay for two agents, it is a solution that allows the owner to agree to 'charterers' agents' in the charter party, yet maintain some degree of control over the vessel's port call. This is particularly true in cases where the owner has a hub agent who will then be responsible for disbursing funds locally.

This is a unique and complex area of agency practice and deserves further detailed study.

# Chapter 15
## Managing a Tramp Ship Agency

The agent who is strictly tramp is usually in a situation of feast or famine. There are either too many ships or not enough in any given week, month or year. Tramp agency is unpredictable, even with contracted principals. Therefore, staffing and fixed costs must be carefully measured to match slow cycles. Cost control is extremely important and all employees must be vigilant.

## 15.1    Tramp Agency Fees

Tramp ship agency remuneration is made up of a base agency fee for services plus a list of recoverable expenses. The agent must have a well managed system for cost recovery which can handle communication expenses, transportation and other items for each individual ship. Close cooperation between the accounting department and operations department when calculating agency fees will improve the firm's revenue. The best approach is to determine the cost and profit required on a ship by ship basis. The accounting department can help greatly in this effort and their advice should be sought.

In some countries, the agency fees are established by a shipping association and are usually the minimum recommended fees. Many agents consult this tariff when quoting agency fees to ship owners. In many cases, they are requested to negotiate a lower fee to be competitive with other agents in the marketplace. Usually a compromise is reached.

Every ship agency has its own system for calculating remuneration, which includes agency fees, recovery of expenses and extra service charges. The structure of the agency remuneration would be agency fees determined by the size of the ship or cargo handled for the first three or five days in port. If the ship remains in port beyond the first three or five days, there is a daily fee charged. Where the ship will discharge and then backload, there will be an extra agency fee charged for the second charter party for the vessel to load. This fee will usually be less than the first discharge fee, as a courtesy to the ship owner.

An owner's or charterer's protecting agency fee will be less than for full service, reflecting the smaller workload. If it is a charterer's protecting agency the agent will be focused only on the cargo operation, not the husbanding. If it is an owner's protecting agency, the agent will be tasked with performing husbanding services and supervision of the actions of the agent that the ship owner was compelled to appoint in accordance with the charter party terms.

The owner's husbanding agency service is where the agent attends only to the husbanding needs of a ship while it is in the hands or control of another agent. This could also apply where the vessel is calling off of the port limits, for bunkers, spare parts delivery or emergency crew changes.

# 15.2   Service Fees

## 15.2.1   Spare parts handling service fees

This service fee would be for handling the coordination of the collection, clearance and delivery of spare parts to the ship. It could also cover handling from the ship to the airport and arranging the export brokerage of the spare parts. This is usually charged on a per pallet or per airway bill basis. The agent's fee for handling spare parts will be on top of the cost of paying for customs clearance for the spare parts at the airport, as well as transportation to the ship.

## 15.2.2   Crew change service fees

This service involves arranging for visas and meeting and greeting arriving crew at the airport. It may also involve arranging hotels and transportation to and from the ship. This fee is usually charged on a per seafarer basis or, where there are multiple crew changes, there will be a flat fee for the first three, the first five, the first ten, etc. In these cases, the agent's fee will be on top of the cost of car services, hotels, food and visas.

## 15.2.3   Agent expense recovery

The agent's expenses include the cost of transportation, domestic communication, satellite communication with the vessel, customs' bonding, customs' forms, cost to deliver cash to the Master and any other expenses the agent would incur to attend the ship that were unique to the port where the agent was domiciled.

There could also be special fees for attending to general average, medical emergencies, dry docking services, etc.

## 15.2.4   Calculating agency fees

When calculating compensation, the agent should first determine the actual costs to handle the particular type of ship. One possible method would be to determine the total cost of running the port agency per year and then determining the cost per hour for it to operate. As tramp vessels usually stay in port for short periods of time, which can be measured in hours, knowing the cost per hour and adding on top of that cost plus profit is a simple guideline to determine how agency fees could be calculated.

This would be particularly useful where the ship owner requires the agents to quote his remuneration on a lump sum basis.

## 15.2.5 Lump sum agency fees

Lump sum remuneration is of interest to the ship owner because, when reviewing the final disbursement account, they do not have to review in detail each item of the agent's service and expenses for government blankforms, petty cash, postage, transportation, communication, crew changes, spare parts handling, etc. There is a flat remuneration amount. This also makes it easier for the principal to compare agents' costs when agents are competing against each other. The problem that lump sum agency fees pose to the agents is that, if they are not careful, they will end up negotiating against themselves. The agent must know exactly what his operating costs are to handle each individual ship. The cost will be approximate as any ship can stay longer than expected. When negotiating lump sum agency fees, you can indicate to the owner that the lump sum fee is based upon so many days in port, with minimal or routine husbanding requirements. Any extra days beyond the first set will be charged on a per diem basis. Likewise, any crew handling beyond the first four would also be charged as an extra amount, and any spares after the first shipment would be an extra fee.

> When negotiating the agency fee, it is important that the agent has a walk away number. This means that, if the agency in negotiation with the ship owner is approaching the break even mark to handle the ship, sometimes it is best just to walk away from it. One ship agent told me that they were once presented with the opportunity to handle upwards of three port calls a week at an oil refinery, but the agency compensation was low. The agent's response to me was, "why do I want to take on a whole new business that's only going to be break even?" The agent was already profitable with the number of ships he was handling. More port calls do not necessarily mean more profits. There is a cost associated with additional ships.

## 15.2.6 Charterer's agents provided competitive

For a voyage charter nomination, the charter party might read:

*"charterer's nominated agent at the port, vessel paying customary port charges and agency fee provided competitive".*

The intention of this clause is to prevent the voyage charterer's nominated agent from charging the ship owner excessively high remuneration just because the owner is compelled to use them. However, the reverse has taken place. Ship owners are getting bids from other agents, or using their own agency relationship with a certain agent, to challenge the voyage charterer's nomination as being uncompetitive. This poses a difficult situation for ship agents, who have to negotiate with the ship owner who is challenging them with an agency fee that they have with an established agent that they regularly give ships to.

The Association of Ship Brokers and Agents in the United States has encouraged owners to change the words to 'provided customary and reasonable' rather than 'provided competitive'. Customary and reasonable directs the owner and the agent to the prevailing agency fees within the marketplace of that port normally charged by an agent handling a spot ship. Where the owner is being unreasonable in his negotiations with the charterer's nominated agent, this situation will revert back to the voyage charterer to settle. In some cases, an oil company will inform an owner that the agency fee being charged by their nominated agent is the same agency fee that the agent charges them. This usually puts an end to the dispute.

### 15.2.7 Cruise ship agency fees

When handling cruise ships, the agent will deal with three or four different departments within the company. The port operations department will negotiate a lump sum agency fee with the agent. The cost of handling spare parts to and from the ship and the agent's fee for that service will go to the technical department. The agent's fee for handling crew changes goes to the personnel department.

### 15.2.8 Outstanding disbursement accounts

It is common practice for ship owners to remit to agents 80-90% of the requested advance disbursements. The owners do this on the assumption that the agent overestimates the port costs to take into consideration any possible extra husbanding requirements of the ship. The ship owners remit a lesser amount than requested because they want to reduce the volume of funds they have outstanding from cash flow. Furthermore, the owners believe that reducing the amount of funds requested by the agent will encourage them to speed up processing of the disbursement account and have it sent more quickly to settle the voyage cost. All of these assumptions are correct. However, in some instances the amount outstanding can be fairly large. Consider, for example, a US$3,000.00 outstanding balance from a port call. It will take the agent approximately 30-40 days to finalize the disbursement account and submit it to the ship owner. It may take the ship owner another 30-40 days to process the disbursement account and be prepared to remit the balance of funds due to the agent. In this example, under the best of circumstances, the agent is looking at financing $2-3,000.00 for a 90 day period. Because the agent is compelled to pay all port costs in a timely fashion, he will incur financing charges to pay the owner's expenses in port. In a situation like this, the agent should consider advising the ship owner clearly on the disbursement account that there is a finance charge on the balance due after a set number of days. The finance charge can be determined by the normal charges for business lines of credit at the bank where the agent is domiciled. An administrative fee may also be added by the agent.

> Although this may be difficult to collect, it is possible that the agent may be able to do this in an effort to reduce his costs of financing his service of the owner's expenses in port.

# 15.3   Accounting

> **Accounting is the most vulnerable part of any tramp agency. Many agents will tell you that the majority of complaints from principals are due to accounting errors When management makes the effort to have the operations department and the accounting department work in close harmony, a mutual understanding and cooperation develops.**

The best tramp agents are those that have the most active and concerned accounting department handling the operations disbursement accounts. More principals are lost by an agent due to accounting problems than for any other reason.

Accounting is also the last point of communication between the agent and the ship owner. No matter how well the marine operations are performed, if the accounting of ship's disbursements is late or poorly presented, or if accounting staff do not respond quickly to enquiries, the principal's disappointment will reflect on the whole firm. The most common problem in tramp agency is the operations department blaming all their disbursement account problems on the accounts department. That is never correct as the accounting and operations departments are equal partners in the provision of the tramp ship agency services. Operations staff who do not actively cooperate with their accounting counterparts are leaving the job half done.

The balance of cash flow through accounts receivable and accounts payable is very important and must be carefully managed. It has an impact that goes beyond the financial statements. In many countries, ship agents are held liable for the principal's debts, and so port authorities and agents will not permit a ship to berth or leave until the full amount of estimated disbursements has been received by the agent. Where this requirement does not exist, it is just as important to ensure that the correct amount of funds has been received before the ship sails. However, it is still possible for the expenses to exceed the funds advanced. Under these circumstances, it is most important that the ship operator receives the accounting of the port of call as soon as possible after the ship's departure. Many agents now send a summary of expenses immediately after the ship sails. The faster the owner receives the disbursement account, the sooner the settlement can be made. This quick dispatch provides a good service to the ship owner and, at the same time, allows aggressive control of the accounts receivable.

As important as accounts receivable is accounts payable. The agent's credibility and reputation in a port are often a reflection of how quickly vendors and port authorities are paid after a service is rendered to the ship. This is often a criteria by which an owner will judge the selection of a new agency in any area.

> **Accounting plays an important role in both service reputation and market perception of the agent. Principals have been known to contact pilots, tug companies, stevedores and other service providers in a port to determine an agent's financial credibility. If these people**

**and firms do not give a positive response, the principal may take the view that the agency has financial problems or is mismanaged.**

### 15.3.1   When a balance of funds is due back to the principal

When the agent has a surplus of funds remaining, every effort should be made to remit the funds back to the principal as soon as possible. Some owners accuse agents of trying to steal the owner's money by withholding it. This is usually not the case. In most final disbursement accounts, a cover letter is written requesting the owner to revert with their banking details to send back the funds. However, this sometimes gets ignored. Tramp accounting managers should not hold funds for 'when the ship returns'. This assumes the owners want to have a running account. Most owners prefer to have all accounts settled on a voyage by voyage basis and not have funds comingled.

## 15.4   Communications

Communication is the most important aspect of the tramp agent's service.

Far too many ship agents do not communicate enough with their principals. The worst example are those agents who fail to answer an email the same day. The agent must be aware of time zone differences, and ensure that a response goes to the principal in the principal's business hours. If that is not possible, then at least a response should be sent during the agent's business day. If for some reason a full response is not possible, receipt of the correspondence should be acknowledged and the principal informed when a detailed response will be made with an explanation of why the information may not be available at the time.

Another fault occurs when a ship is idle in port or waiting berthing. Often, the agent will not send an email to the principal, thinking that yesterday's email forecasting no activity today will suffice. It will not. At least say something to the principal, if only to confirm that nothing has happened and nothing is scheduled for the next day, with an explanation.

The telephone can be the agent's best friend and worst enemy. Too often an agent will answer the telephone as if they have just run a marathon. This alarms the principal, as it creates the impression that the agent is too busy to attend to the principal's needs. However, a worse situation arises when a principal cannot contact the agent by telephone. Every agent should remember that, if the principal cannot contact you, you become non-existent, you are out of contact and you might as well be out of business. This is particularly the case when trying to reach an agent out of office hours.

Communication is vital and must be constantly tested, evaluated and, if possible, upgraded. The best ship agencies have a system of rules and regulations for all communications. These firms review their communications efficiency regularly to avoid the situation of becoming 'non-existent' to the client.

> **Agents should communicate at least twice a day with the principal, at open of business and close of business locally. If there are no changes, then state so.**

Handheld email devices are common today and it is important that the agent communicates in a clear and easily readable format, with a very concise subject matter showing the vessel name and port. If the principal cannot easily identify your email when checking his email, his first impression is that the agent has sent no updates.

When communicating with a new principal, the agent must exercise concern to ensure his emails are not going into 'spam'. To avoid this, it might be worthwhile making a courtesy call to the principal to verify that they are receiving your email in a timely fashion.

If the ship owner emails or contacts the agent in any way asking for an update on the ship's position, there is something wrong. If the principal has to ask the agent for an update then the agent must consider that they are not doing their job properly and they are failing in their communication obligations.

> **The worst thing that can happen is for your customer's boss to ask them what is going on, and they have to report that they haven't heard from the agent.**

When the agent is asked questions, it is best to acknowledge receipt of the enquiry. Report when you will be able to take action and when you expect to report back. If you are unable to get the information within the time stated, inform the principal about what is delaying the information. Give the new date and time that the information is going to be provided. The worst thing the agent can do is to say nothing. The principal has no idea whether you are taking action or not.

The most important thing the agent must remember about communication is that if the principal hasn't heard from you, they are assuming you are not doing your business, that you are not taking care of the ship, or that you forgot the ship is in port. In summary, you are not doing your job and the ship operator's opinion of your service will reflect that.

## 15.4.1 Port costs requests

It is always best to acknowledge that you have received the request and to confirm when you will respond. In the response, show how the cost estimate was calculated with a supporting narrative. The narrative is to explain your assumptions, for example the number of tugs used, if tugs used in overtime, berthing delays, etc. Also include the current berth lineup and the port and berth restrictions. It is prudent to telephone the party making the enquiry the next day to confirm that they received your information, answer any questions and determine whether they had fixed the business. If they do not fix the business then ask who did. This is a perfect example to market your services to this principal. It is acceptable to ask the inquiring party who secured the business if they didn't.

## 15.4.2  Communication recommendations

When communicating with a principal, always include your name and contact details at the end of every email.

When communicating, never press 'reply all' unless you know exactly who all the parties are on the recipient list. When in doubt, ask the principal to confirm whether these people are eligible to receive your communication.

 **If everyone hits 'reply all' in a trail of communication, it is possible for parties to receive your communication who should not.**

When dealing with a principal, always be cognizant of the time zone where they live.

Tell your principal everything and never withhold information describing what is going on. In the case of berthing prospects, if there are none, tell the principal what the terminal told you, even if it is reporting that the terminal refuses to announce to anyone what their berthing schedule is in advance. Tell the principal the name of the person who told you this.

If there is a problem and you are coordinating this with the Master, you must also keep the principal updated on the progress. You must inform the principal or the head office or home office for the ship what the problem is and what action you are taking to solve it. This must be reported on a regular basis, perhaps at least twice a day. If the principal is not getting the updates from the agent, then the agent is losing control of the principal's perception of the agent's good effort. Do not leave it to the Master or third parties to provide updates on your progress solving a problem.

**In certain countries, the boarding agents do not have handheld communication devices or cellular telephones with the capacity to make international phone calls. They must wait until they return to the office to send arrival information and report back to the principals. Most principals have handheld devices. If you are unable to communicate with the principal, your competition will be way ahead of you.**

Today, most ships have the capacity for satellite communications by email, telex, fax and telephone. An agent is wise never to assume that the Master or visiting superintendent or cargo expeditor is doing the communications and updating your principal. That is the job of the ship agent. If those individuals are sending updates because they're obligated to do so, that's well and good. However, it does not excuse the agent from providing timely reports at least once or twice daily

# 15.5   Staffing

This is one of the most difficult matters to manage. Due to the uncertainty of port calls, the tramp agent needs just the right number of people in order to be both efficient and profitable.

Some of the more common complaints principals have against agents come from the Master, who claims to have seen the agent only rarely during the ship's time in port. This may be true if there are insufficient staff or no system to ensure adequate service.

Another staffing problem occurs when there are plenty of people available, but the only person who knows what is going on with a particular ship is out of the office and unavailable.

If either of these situations happens, it is an indication that there is no system of service to the principal. If a principal cannot speak to the agent to obtain up to date information, the agent might as well be closed for the day.

If the agency has insufficient staff, the employees become exhausted from working around the clock for days on end without free time. Periods of high ship volume are common and, if the agency is understaffed in average periods, the service of the agent can collapse very quickly when the volume picks up. If this happens, the agent's credibility and reputation also collapse. Once an agent loses its reputation, either because of poor service or low staff morale, it is almost impossible to win back the trust of principals. One lost principal usually means other lost principals, as ship owners talk together and they will not only recommend who they would use, but also who they wouldn't.

It is difficult to keep port agency staff in many countries. Port agency is difficult and there is too much competition for other careers. The best way to retain staff is to keep them interested. Money isn't the only source of retention. Invite boarding agents and operations managers to make sales calls. Have them attend entertainment with visiting principals' representatives. If the agency belongs to shipping associations or social and service organizations, have the staff actively involved. It will be a reward for them and their spouses if they can attend these social functions.

Another key issue is staff education. Provide staff with news articles, trade publications and updates on changes of regulations. Highlight magazine and trade publication articles about the principals.

Always try to find ways to reduce the stress on staff and their family life, for example extended vacations and long holiday weekends. Use alternate holidays and weekends among the staff so no one person is working all the time. This is particularly the case if they really want to work all the time to gather overtime pay, if that is allotted to them.

Allow staff access to updated technology to make their job easier, for example internet access from home, smart phones or other mobile communication devices to enable them to have international communications.

Tramp agents are judged on a ship by ship basis and are only as good as the most recent service provided. Therefore, the agent must create a system of service that maintains continuity and consistency of service.

# Chapter 16
## Tramp Ship Agency Marketing

> **There are many sources of guidance on establishing a marketing program.**

This chapter outlines some of our experiences and observations on the tramp agency business, and suggests methods of marketing tramp agency services which may help the small or mid-size ship agency sales efforts.

The tramp agency depends upon ship volume to cover operating costs and create a profit. Therefore, the agent must develop a significant number of potential principals, such as ship operators, voyage charterers, shippers and receivers, from whom to derive ship agency appointments.

Most of the large ship agencies cover many ports of a geographic region and the global agency networks have professionally trained sales teams to do their marketing. The sales teams are located in major shipping centers around the world.

The great equalizer in tramp agency is that, for the most part, charterers and ship operators are seeking dedicated service that is consistent, attentive and reasonably priced. Therefore, the one-port ship agent will have the same ability to compete for new business on a one on one basis as a large corporation at that single port. The key to success is the ability to determine the type of agency service the principal is truly seeking. There are an equal number of potential principals who prefer the larger organization as there are those who prefer to select the agent one port at a time, based upon the skill and knowledge of the individual at the port.

No matter the size of the agency, you must know your business and who you derive your business from. There are a surprising number of tramp agents who are unable to determine from whom and why the agency appointments are coming. The agent must differentiate a voyage charter nomination from an operator's appointment. Defining the source of the agency appointments by operators and voyage charterers is important if you are to be aware of trends, potential vulnerabilities as well as for financial management. This knowledge also determines sales and marketing strategies for each port and the company as a whole.

The agent must also be aware if any one principal represents a significant percentage of his total revenue. If this situations exist, a marketing strategy to diversify the customer base is necessary.

> Each company should have its own system to monitor progress in monthly financial reports. However, avoid the temptation to become overwhelmed by too many reports and analyses. The function of analysis is to tell you where you came from, where you are now and to establish a plan for the future growth of the company, as well as to monitor the success of the marketing strategy.

An important aspect of the tramp agency is new business development and current principal maintenance. Principal maintenance requires routine visits or, at least, telephone contact by management to determine service and satisfaction, market trends, development within the principal's organization in an effort to define new services in order to increase revenue. New business development is a slow process. Tramp principals, ship operators and charterers alike are not inclined to change agents with any frequency.

> The best philosophy for a tramp agency is that new principals cannot be developed unless they know you and trust you. Tramp agents don't lose principals; the agents give the principals away to their competition. Simply stated, a principal will continue to support a good agent if he sees that the agent is paying attention to, show concern for his interests. An agent cannot gain the confidence of new principals unless he stays in contact, even at a time when they are not handling the principal's ship. Therefore, the agent must travel on a regular basis to visit important principals and potential principals to discuss new business.

If they do not see you, they will forget you.

When establishing your sales and marketing, consider the following:

* It is cheaper to keep an existing customer than it is to find a new customer
* initially, any new principal takes 6-9 months to develop before the first ship assignment
* tramp principals tend to judge the new agent one port call at a time.

The first appointment by a new principal does not imply support of the agent's total network. Each time the new principal expands the relationship with the agent at another port, they should be viewed as if they were a new principal at that port. The objective of tramp sales is to continue developing the relationship with each principal until they embrace the agent's total network.

The relationship between the tramp principal and the agent is not normally contractual. Therefore, routine contact and, when possible, visits to the principal are necessary to maintain continued support and expansion of the relationship to all ports of the agent's network.

It is important to be associated with the major commodities importers and exporters of the port. Shippers and receivers have influence on the agency that the owners must appoint under voyage charters.

Targeting and prospecting by commodity for a charterer's nomination can be effective. Voyage charter nominations produce the highest revenue per ship. To gain recognition in any commodity, it is helpful to have at least one principal to use for reference and referrals.

A sales program where quick results are needed in the short term should allow the marketing plan to concentrate on the market the agency is most familiar with. However, it is prudent not to chase a short-term strategy for too long as it may detract from company objectives for other ports or commodities.

Rigidly adhering only to assigned targets does not always produce results and diverting to chase leads and assumptions can often be successful. A lead should be followed up until the business is secured or the opportunity ceases to exist, then return to your target account list and resume your marketing plan.

> **The local operations managers should be encouraged to participate by generating leads and, where necessary, to make sales calls. However, not all operations people make good sales people. Some people are not comfortable in this situation. The worst thing a manager can do is to force the operations person into a sales presentation. The most gregarious operations manager on the phone in the office might have stage fright when placed in the prospective principal's office to make a sales representation. Remember that the reason for the individual's continued employment is their skill as an operations manager. If they are unable or unwilling to do something they are not comfortable with, do not force them to be something they were not hired for.**

It is important that the agent's management recognize the sales person's authority to recommend the implementation of quality controls at the local port level and to work with accounting services to maintain principals and adjust to the needs of new principals. A large part of tramp sales is the presentation of yourself as a tramp agent who can equally serve the charterer or the ship owner in specific commodity trades.

> **Good tramp agency service encourages repeat business, but not forever – only until a better offer is made or a change takes place within the staff of the principal or agent. To retain current principals, the agent must avoid complacency and assume that the competition also make sales calls and regular visits to these principals. Remember, it is less costly to keep existing customers and to expand that relationship than it is to develop new customers.**

Sales is a percentage game and there will more often be a 'no' than a 'yes'. New business development is an ongoing process and it is difficult to have any success with a start and stop program. If you are busy 'doing the business' and providing the service, try to set aside a little bit of time for marketing each week - at least one phone call or perhaps a meeting. Whatever you can do is better than doing nothing. Generally, the more sales calls made that are properly followed up, the better the results. Persistence and follow up is the key to success.

## 16.1   Selling to an Owner

> **In our experience, ship owners don't always trust ship agents. This might be because, under a voyage charter, they are compelled to employ someone they do not necessarily know in a foreign country and to give them a large sum of money in the hope that it is used wisely.**

Another concern is the financial security of the agent. Many owners have been burned by having to pay disbursements twice. Make sure that your presentation illustrates your financial security.

Owners often bemoan the failure of the voyage charterer's nominated agent to keep them advised of what is occurring while the ship is in the agent's care. The same applies to the simple things such as arrival and repatriation of crew and delivery of spare parts. Email confirmation of crew arrival or departure is a small detail that can leave a favorable impression.

The dispatch of the statement of facts and sending all documents electronically immediately after sailing while having the original documents dispatched by courier within 24 hours after sailing is crucial, particularly when you consider demurrage time bar clauses. This is expected by the charterers as well as the owners.

To be more than just a port agent, you must do little things that show you are making the extra effort to be aware of the particular needs of an owner.

Acting as an owner's agent is something that ship agents are most familiar with. However, selling to owners becomes complex as you must say something that will interest them more than what your competition says.

Furthermore you must always bear in mind the owner's commercial concerns and convey this appreciation to the owner. It is recommended that you demonstrate value added services such as cost saving initiatives where possible.

The presentation to the ship owner should outline standard operating procedures such as daily communications, visiting the ship, and observing and reporting cargo operations. Depending upon the size of your company, list the operations staff by title and years of experience in shipping. Offer a brief indicative list of your principals. Finally, give examples of your cost saving and time saving skills and accomplishments.

Your presentation must be brief so that it does not lose the interest of the person you are meeting. Ask the prospect how they pick agents and what they like about the agents they use and compare that with what you do. The more the ship owner talks, the higher the probability they will feel that this was a good meeting. The more you talk, the less success you will have. Finally, before leaving the meeting, ask for the business. Ask for at least one trial agency appointment.

 **Do not leave without asking for the business.**

No matter how bad you feel the meeting was, always ask for the business. That is why you are there. The owner expects you to ask the question.

# 16.2    Selling to a Charterer

Selling to a charterer is very different from selling to an owner. The charterer places a lot of demands on the agent simply by the fact of having to coordinate the contract of carriage, the contract of sale and their relationship with their customer at the port. The faster the cargo is loaded or discharged, the faster the trader collects his money under the letter of credit

The operations manager, traffic manager or chartering manager for a trader is under great pressure from the actual traders to keep voyage costs down, while keeping trade opportunities open. Therefore, the agent is expected to keep the charterer updated without having to be asked.

To be successful, the agent must have a good understanding of the commodity the charterer deals with, knowledge of the inland transportation, quality and quantity controls of the product, and the terms and conditions of the charter party used in the trade.

To sell to a charterer you should stress the strengths of your tramp agency, but expand from there by showing your method of operation is sympathetic to the special commercial concerns of the charterer and their customers.

The charterer is concerned with your communication procedures and skill at handling documentation. Preparing B/Ls and other documents accurately and quickly is often a key requirement. They will want to know whether your staff are experienced with their commodity. The communication issue is unique for the voyage charterer. They need to receive updates on the cargo operations around the clock. You should have a good working relationship with the shipper or receiver as well as with the terminal operations manager where the cargo will be handled.

> When selling to the person who controls the selection of the agency you must sell to that person's pressures and demonstrate how your understanding enables you to meet their needs through your specialized tramp agency service.

# 16.3    Planning a Sales Call

Always remember that you are selling to a person who has a boss. Commodity traders continually ask their ship brokers for rates and demand explanations of why the ship isn't performing as expected. The chartering department for a ship owner or a ship operator is always demanding operational updates, port costs, port condition and productivity of the ship under charter. To develop new tramp agency business, the agent must be innovative in addressing the specific needs of the individual in the principal's employment.

## 16.3.1    The nuisance factor

> When working with people who are under constant pressure and stress, any extra time or effort the agent imposes is a deterrent to using that agent again.

It is a nuisance for the principal if he has to ask you for an update on the operations, to clarify an explanation, or to request documentation, particularly if he cannot reach you immediately or doesn't get an acknowledgment or response from you to his communication. Each of these situations creates extra work. It's a nuisance.

## 16.3.2    Other sales call recommendations

> When planning a sales call or a maintenance meeting with a new or established principal, always request the meeting in writing and then follow up with a telephone call. Send written confirmation that the meeting has been accepted on the date and time you discussed.

Arrive at the meeting location five minutes before the meeting is scheduled to begin. Although in some cultures it is inappropriate to arrive early, this does allow you time to review your notes before going into the meeting. <u>Never be late.</u>

Make every effort not to waste the time of the person you are visiting. For a new customer, assume no more than a 45 minute meeting unless the person takes interest in your service. When scheduling sales calls for the day, allow sufficient time between sales calls.

Turn off your cell phone.

Wear a suit and tie or appropriate business attire for the city which you're visiting.

Present business cards and a brochure about your company.

Do your homework before the meeting. Make a point to know what the company does, where they do it, and with whom they do it. Don't schedule something without knowing exactly why you're there and what that company does.

Before entering the building, read through all the names again so you pronounce each name correctly. Read through your notes as to why you're there and what you intend to accomplish.

Take notes during the meeting. It shows the principal you are interested in what he has to say. However, do not take copious notes so it appears you are taking dictation. Never use your own corporation's sales call report form to fill in the blanks during your sales call.

Write a sales call presentation and memorize it. Follow up each sales call with a short note of thanks. Even if you've seen the person many times before, a simple sentence to say thank you for your time is more than enough. If follow up is required, state in your message that you're following up on their enquiry and will revert soon.

Carry breath mints and be cognizant of your own personal hygiene.

 **Do not leave without asking for the business. That is why you are there.**

# Chapter 17
## The Tramp Ship Agency Career
----------------------------------------

If a student were presented with a book of careers, providing complete job descriptions, we believe tramp ship agency would be among the last choices. The reasons are simple: unsocial hours, low pay, non-professional social status and high pressure.

Tramp ships have no schedule, so arrival and departure and loading and discharge may be at any time. In most ports a tanker will load or discharge without the constraint of normal business hours, weekends or holidays. Although many dry cargo voyage charterers are affected by local labor rules, the ship's port arrival and departure can occur at any time, day or night, weekend or holiday. Therefore, the boarding agent must be present at those times, for both the tanker and the dry cargo tramp ships.

It is not uncommon for a boarding agent to meet one ship arriving at port at two o'clock in the morning, depart the ship at five o'clock and then proceed directly to the office for a full day's work. At the end of the day, they may still return to the same ship to witness her sailing at ten o'clock at night.

Considering the importance to a Master, ship owner or cargo interest, and the potential financial damage resulting from an agent's error, it is startling that in many countries tramp agency personnel are not certified or licensed by a government or industry authority. Consequently, ship agents do not receive the professional status or salary of a ship or charter broker. There are a few nations where ship agency is taught on a professional level, such as Germany and England. However, for the most part, tramp ship agency personnel begin as boarding agents or water clerks and promotion is generally based upon the individual's knowledge and enthusiasm for the job. In the USA, the Association of Ship Brokers and Agents USA Inc (ASBA) has established a program to educate current and new agents entering the tramp agency industry. ASBA has created a study guide with basic information about shipping and each candidate must pass a written exam. If successful, the candidate is certified by ASBA as having basic shipping knowledge. This allows an ASBA member to market themselves as having an educated corps of operations staff.

On a global basis, the Federation of National Associations of Ship Brokers and Agents, FONASBA, has instituted the FONASBA Quality Standard. While each member country submits a unique regimen for their members to achieve the Quality Standard, there are certain basic criteria required of all countries, professional training and education among them. The FONASBA Quality Standard is issued to the company, not the individual. The aim of these initiatives is to create an awareness for and recognition of a higher standard of competence within the industry.

Why, therefore, would anyone desire to become and remain associated with tramp ship agency? The reasons are about the same as those for any type of employment. The basic employee needs or motivators are as follows:

- Job security
- sense of satisfaction
- achievement
- recognition of achievement
- responsibility
- advancement
- growth.

In terms of revenue, the tramp agent's fees have not gone up much over the years. By comparison with other voyage costs, the fees are minimal. The tramp agent's fees in some countries have been established and determined by a government or industry authority. Although the agent's fees may be negotiable, the remuneration per ship will not vary as erratically as a liner tariff or a shipbroker's commission. Therefore, assuming a tramp ship volume varies no more than 5-10% annually, revenue and profits will be somewhat steady. This generalization avoids the insecurity of lay-offs, which are common in other marine service sectors.

Tramp ships arrive to conduct cargo operations and can stay in port anywhere from less than a day up to many days, so there is always variety. There is a sense of the finite with every agency consignment, i.e. the ship will eventually leave port. The boarding agent and office staff will be judged by each owner and master. Each staff member is personally aware, at each ship's departure, whether they completed their tasks to the best of their ability. If a vessel sailed without incident, or if any problems that arose were satisfactorily solved, the tramp agency employee will have the feeling of a job well done. Whether or not this is acknowledged by the principal or peers, the individual will be their own best judge and, hopefully, have a sense of satisfaction.

Achievement and, although rarely, recognition of achievement, is anticipated and sought with each new vessel arrival. It is human nature to seek reward. That reward is most gratifying when gained by recognition by a person's peers. The satisfaction from achievement is easily available by the constant turnover of various ships calling at a port and serviced by the agency.

Responsibility and accountability are major characteristics of tramp agency practice. The boarding agent and operations manager work as a team to satisfy the husbanding needs of the ship and all her crew. Concurrently, both the owner and the charterer have large sums of money invested in any voyage. The probability that something will go wrong is always higher in either the load or discharge port, as opposed to at sea. A tramp agent's advice, accurate presentation of facts and, in some cases, negotiating skills have been known to prevent many problems from getting out of control.

The ship's Master is dependent upon the boarding agent to guide him through the complex procedure of ship inspection by government authorities. The owner and charterer rely upon the agent to advise the Master on how to prepare his ship for economical and efficient cargo operations. Furthermore, the owner and Master depend upon the agent to make them aware of channel drafts, bridge clearances and water depths at a berth.

The agent is always delegated by the Master to select reputable shore labor and technicians to carry out ship repairs. Spare parts, sent to the ship by airfreight, must arrive urgently to the ship to avoid sailing delays. Collection and delivery of spare parts is the agent's responsibility.

The timely, efficient and economic coordination of such tasks as the ordering and delivery of stores, provisions, fresh water and bunkers, assisting crew joining or repatriating, repairs to navigation equipment and collecting the Master's wife and children from the airport are all the duty and responsibility of the agent. The agent is accountable for any delay to delivery or completion of these duties. After all, the boarding agent is performing those tasks the Master cannot physically perform, or would be performed if the owner was domiciled at the port.

The extent of the agent's responsibility to give advice and to perform a variety of duties during the short period of a vessel's port call is endless. The agent's most important responsibility to the owner, Master or charterer is to expedite the cargo operations and get the ship back out to sea.

Of all the agent's duties, the timely delivery of mail and cash to the crew is of paramount importance. You are also there to take care of the people on board.

A boarding agent's first lesson is in responsibility and accountability. Failure to apply the extra effort in completing a task can involve a severe reprimand from the Master, ship owner or operations manager.

Every day is different. Every port call will be different. As an agent, you get involved with many aspects of the business including:

- Arranging medical evacuations
- negotiating a solution to an operations problem
- negotiation of a waiver of rules with a government authority
- assisting the Master with personnel problems with crew members
- coordinating emergency repairs.

There are many things an agent does that are greatly appreciated by the Master, owners and charterers. The agent is the problem solver and people will remember your name.

This kind of responsibility is very exciting provided you are up to the challenge. Responsibility and accountability, such as that described above, is one reason why people enter and remain in tramp ship agency.

The ability to think quickly, clearly and calmly during a pressured situation is one of the traits management will seek in young people. Tramp agency employees are exposed to every aspect of shipping. Through this experience and international exposure, a well-rounded and knowledgeable person will develop.

Consciously or unconsciously, people see a ship in port as being under someone's care, usually a ship agent's care. It is as if the agent's name was written in bold letters across the hull. Therefore, the individual boarding agent and the ship agency firm's reputation is on trial for all to see.

Under these circumstances, a boarding agent's skill comes to the attention of his employer's management and the person's peers within the port. If and when an opportunity of advancement becomes available, a boarding agent is often considered a candidate.

> You have to be a special person to be a ship agent. This life is not for everyone. In the office of one of the writer's principals is a photo that the customer took while Master of a VLCC sailing between Alaska and the US West Coast. The photo was taken from the bridge during heavy weather. A massive wave was cresting over the bow of the tanker. At the bottom of the photo was the inscription:

You Gotta Wanna Do This!

# Chapter 18
## Authors' Thoughts

The merger and acquisition period in ship agency has created a consolidation of many tramp agencies into much larger groups, creating national agencies from several regional tramp agencies or, in some cases, adding to existing worldwide groups. The impact upon the principal is generally positive. The principal is presented with an agent who is financially stronger and has more resources, such as increased staffing in each agency port as well as access to more market information and contacts in many other ports and countries.

The unique quality of tramp agency business is the relationship between the principal's operations staff and the agent's operations staff. The principal's position overall has been to support the people at the port level no matter the change in the ownership, management or name of the agency company. Many principals, both owners and charterers, have associated 'my agent' with the individuals at each port, not the company.

In most situations, provided the principals receive at least the same service as prior to the merger or acquisition, they will maintain their support of 'my agents' at each port, no matter what corporate identity it is given.

In most countries, the creation of tramp ship agencies is relatively easy to accomplish. However, this should not be attempted without the support of principals who either charter ships or are shippers or receivers capable of influencing the nomination of the agents. This allows the agent sufficient income to begin the new company and provide the principals with exclusive service.

There is discussion in the industry whether or not the smaller or mid-sized tramp agency can compete against the newly-created global agents who have significant resources for marketing, value added services, large numbers of ports and the ability to comply with the quality management certification required by some major international corporations' selection of vendors and service providers.

Large corporations do not necessarily imply good service, nor do mid-sized or small companies imply lack of creativity and foresight to plan growth or react to the needs of the customers. The tramp agencies that are able to adjust to changes and meet the challenges will survive and grow. The size of the organization does not guarantee success.

Regardless of the changes taking place within the tramp agency business, one constant remains. It is a people business. The agent has few physical assets. The primary strength is the relationship with the principals.

Those of us that work in the industry know that the maritime transportation industry is a small community. Our companies are only as good as the people who work there. A firm can have all the highly educated business management available, but the agent's relationship with an owner, vendor or charterer all boils down to individuals keeping their word.

*"Our word is our bond"*, which is the motto of the London Stock exchange, dating back to at least the 1500s but adopted by the industry, remains the key ingredient to any agency relationship. Once the trust is established, a principal will usually return to support that agent or individual.

To be a ship agent, to live with middle of the night ship arrivals, numerous phone calls, seven day working weeks, long hours, pressure to perform and concurrently maintain a happy home life, you must love the business of shipping. Despite the growth of cynical views of experience and age, most tramp ship agency people reflect upon their jobs and admit that there still remains a sense of adventure that goes along with the association of the sea and the ships. It is a difficult concept to explain to a non-maritime person, who cannot understand why anyone would work such long hours.

We believe the enthusiasm of ship agents is due to the dynamic nature of shipping, where no two days are the same and no two ships are the same. Those associated with shipping appreciate the work and effort required to be successful, and there exists a sense of fraternity among shipping people.

# Bibliography

Alderton, P.M. *Sea Transportation*, 2nd rev. ed., London: Thomas Reed Publications Ltd. 1980. Chapter 1.

Association of Shipbrokers and Agents (USA) Inc, New York. Chapter 15. May 1969, BIMCO Bulletin, May 1969. Chapter 11.

Bannier, F.A.W., "The Ship Agent – his Status and the Law of Agency with regards to the International Convention Relating to "Agents", speaker's paper presented at a one-day seminar held at the Conference Room, Kredietbank, Antwerp, 9 June 1978, London: Lloyd's of London Press Ltd, 1978. Chapter 16.

Bauer, R. Glenn. "Responsibilities of Owner and Charterer to Third Parties – Consequences under Time and Voyage Charters", article submitted to the *Tulane Law Review*, New Orleans: Tulane Law Review Association, Vol. 49, no. 4. May 1975. Chapter 11.

Binder, Ing, Johan, Ph.D. "Duties and Problems of Port Agents", contribution to panel discussion with the general meeting, the Baltic and International Maritime Conference, Copenhagen, May 1981. Copenhagen: BIMCO Bulletin, 1981. Chapter 3.

Buglass, Leslie J. *Marine Insurance and General Average in the United States*, 2nd rev. ed. Centreville: Cornell Maritime Press, 1981. Chapter 2.

Chartered and International Shipbrokers' Protection and Indemnity Club Ltd, *CISBA, Handbook including Protection and Indemnity Rules*, Woking: The Cherry Press Ltd, 1976. Chapter 10.

Cufley, C.F.H. *Ocean Freight and Chartering*, London: Granada Publishing, 1970. Chapter 1, 2, 3, 4, 5.

Eadie, J.D. "Ships' Agency", series of articles reprinted from the pages of *Fairplay International Shipping Weekly*, 23 September 1982 to 8 February 1983, London Fairplay Publications Ltd, 1983. Chapter 5, 11.

Edward, E.J. *Shipbrokers and the Law*, Glasgow: Brown, Son and Ferguson Publishers Ltd, 1957. Chapter 2, 5.

Elden, R.M. *Ship management*, Cambridge: Cornell Maritime Press Inc, 1962. Chapter 2.

Feinberg, Mortimer R., and Tanofsky, Robert, and Tarrant, John J., *The New Psychology for Managing People*, Englewood Cliffs, New Jersey: Prentice-Hall Inc, 1982. Chapter 17.

Gilmore, Grant and Black, Charles L., Jr, *The Law of Admiralty*, 2nd rev, ed. Mineola: The Foundation Press Inc, 1975. Chapter 2.

Healy, Nicolas, J., and Sharpe, David J., *Admiralty Cases and Materials,* St. Paul: West Publishing Co, 1974. Chapter 7.

Ihre, Rolf, and Gorton, Lars, and Sandevarn, Arne. *Shipbrokering and Chartering Practice* London: Lloyd's of London Press Ltd, 1980. Chapter 1.

Kendall, Lane C. *The Business of Shipping,* 4th rev. ed., Centreville: Cornell Maritime Press, 1983. Chapter 1, 2, 3, 4.

Marton, G.S. *Tanker Operations,* Centreville: Cornell Maritime Press, 1979. Chapter 2.

Micali, Paul J. *The Lacy Techniques of Salesmanship,* New York: Hawthorn Books, 1971. Chapter 16.

Packard, William V. *Timechartering,* London: Fairplay Publications Ltd, 1980. Chapter 11.

SMA No. 2178 (Arb. N.Y. 5 December 1985). Chapter 14.

Schiffman, Stephan. *The 25 Sales Strategies.* Holbrook: Adams Media Corp, 1999 Chapter 16.

*Scrutton on Charterparties and Bills of Lading,* 18th rev. ed., Mocatta, A.A. Mustill, M.T., Boyd, S.C., London: Sweet and Maxwell Ltd, 1978. Chapter 6.

Sell, W. Edward. *Sell on Agency,* New York: The Foundation Press Inc, 1975. Chapter 1, 6, 8, 9.

Sembler, William. Professor of Advanced Chartering Problems I, State University of New York, Maritime College, New York, lecture, 27 August 1982 and 19 September 1982. Chapter 3.

Trowbridge, Charles L. "The History, Development and Characteristics of the Charter Concept", article submitted to the *Tulane Law Review,* New Orleans: Tulane Law Review Association, vol. 49, no. 4, May 1975. Chapter 11.

Van Berkum, J.M. and Schuring, W. *Shipping Agency Practice,* 2nd rev. ed., Rotterdam: Educational Foundation for the Port Transport Industry, 1981. Chapter 4.

Vandevernter, Branden. "Analysis of Basic Provisions of the Voyage and Time Charter Parties", article submitted to the *Tulane Law Review,* New Orleans: Tulane Law Review Association, vol. 49, no., 4, May 1975. Chapter 11.

## Cases referred to

*Interocean Shipping Company v National Shipping and Trading Corporation,* 1975 A.M.C. 1283 (2nd Cir. 1975).

*Tarstar Shipping Company v Centuries Ship Line Ltd,* 1979 A.M.C. 1096 (2nd Cir. 1979).

*Minturn v Maynard,* 58 US (17 How.) 477 (1855).

*Exxon Corp v Central Gulf Lines, Inc,* 500 US 603 (1991).

*The S/T Athena, SMA No.* 2178 (1985).

*The Nova Caledonia, SMA No.* 4066 (2010).

# Abbreviations

**A**

| | |
|---|---|
| AA | Always afloat |
| AAAA | Always afloat, always accessible |
| ABS | American Bureau of Shipping |
| ADCOMM | Address Commission |
| AG | Arabian Gulf (used when vessels are proceeding to Arabian ports) (see PG) |
| AGW | All going well |
| AMS | Automated manifest system |
| APIS | Automated passenger information system, which is the CBP system that collects the crew and/or passenger data from the eNOA/D. |
| APS | Arrival pilot station |
| ASBA | Association of Ship Brokers and Agents (USA) Inc |
| ATDNS | Any time day or night (SHINC) |
| ATUTC - HTUTC | Actual time used to count (in relation to laytime) – half time used to count |

**B**

| | |
|---|---|
| B/L | Bill of lading |
| B/N | Booking note |
| BBB | Before breaking bulk |
| BBL | Barrel |
| BCM | Bow to center of manifold |
| BENDS | Both ends (i.e. load and discharge ports) |
| BIMCO | Baltic and International Maritime Council |
| BSW | Bottom sediment and water - impurities in a petroleum cargo |

**C**

| | |
|---|---|
| C and F | Cost and freight |
| C/P or CP | Charter party |
| CA | Central America (i.e. WCCA, or ECCA depending which side) |
| CBFT – CBM | Cubic feet – cubic meters |
| CBP | Customs & Border Protection, combines the services previously performed by the Department of Customs, Immigration and Naturalization Service and the inspections arm of the Department of Agriculture |
| CBT | Clean ballast tanks |
| CHOPT | Charterers' option |
| CIF | Cost, insurance and freight |
| COB | Close of business |
| COGSA | Carriage of Goods by Sea Act |

| | |
|---|---|
| COW | Crude oil washing |
| CPP | Clean petroleum products |
| CQD | Customary quick despatch |
| CRISTAL | Contract Regarding an Interim Supplement to Tanker Liability for Oil Pollution |
| CSO | Company security officer |

**D**

| | |
|---|---|
| DA | Disbursement account |
| DAP | Days all purposes (total time for loading and discharging) Also di-ammonium phosphate, a common fertilizer |
| DEL | Delivery |
| DEM | Demurrage |
| DES | Despatch |
| DLOSP | Dropping last outward sea pilot |
| DOC | Document of compliance |
| DOP | Dropping outward pilot |
| DPP | Dirty petroleum products |
| DRI | Direct reduced iron |
| DWAT | Deadweight all told |
| DWCC | Deadweight cargo capacity |
| DWT | Deadweight |

**E**

| | |
|---|---|
| ECI | East Coast India, contrast with WCI – West Coast India |
| EIU | Even if used |
| eNOA/D | Electronic notice of arrival or departure |
| ETA, B, C, D, R | Estimated time of arrival, berthing, completion, departure, readiness |

**F**

| | |
|---|---|
| FAC | Fast as can |
| FAS | Free alongside |
| FC | Full cargo |
| FDD | Freight, demurrage and defense (a type of insurance for legal expenses available from a P&I club) |
| FEU | Forty foot container equivalent units |
| FHEX - FHINC | Fridays and holidays excluded – included |
| FIO, FIOS, FIOT | Free in and out; free in, out and stowed; free in, out and trimmed |
| FO | Free out; fuel oil; or firm offer (depends on context) |
| FOB | Free on board |
| FOW | First open water |
| FW | Fresh water |
| FWAD/FWDD | Fresh water arrival draft/fresh water departure draft |

**G**

| | |
|---|---|
| GA | General average |
| GLESS | Gearless - a ship that has no (gear) for loading/discharging |

| | |
|---|---|
| GO | Gas oil (fuel similar to, but usually more expensive than, marine diesel oil) |
| GRT | Gross registered tons or tonnage |
| **H** | |
| H and M | Hull and machinery |
| HBI | Hot briqetted iron |
| HHDW | Heavy handy deadweight (scrap) |
| HSS | Heavy grains, soybeans and sorghums |
| **I** | |
| IACS | International Association of Classification Societies |
| ICB | International customs bond |
| IFO | Intermediate fuel oil |
| IGS | Inert gas system |
| ILOW | In lieu of weighing |
| IMO | International Maritime Organization |
| INL | International Navigation Limits (formerly Institute Warranty Limits) |
| ISM | International Safety Management Code |
| ISPS | International Ship and Port Facility Security Code |
| ISSC | International Ship Security Certificate |
| ITF | International Transport Workers Federation |
| **L** | |
| L/C | Letter of credit; or laydays/canceling |
| LASH | Lighter aboard ship (a barge carrying vessel) |
| LBP | Length between perpendiculars |
| LD | Load |
| LNG | Liquefied natural gas |
| LOA | Length overall |
| LOI | Letter of indemnity, Letter of intent |
| LOT | Load on top |
| LPG | Liquefied petroleum gas |
| LS | Lumpum (freight) |
| LSFO | Low sulphur fuel oil |
| LT/MT | Long ton - 2240 pounds |
| | Metric ton - 1000 kilograms or 2204.6223 pounds |
| **M** | |
| MARAD | Maritime Administration (branch of US government concerned with shipping) |
| MARPOL | The International Convention for Prevention of Pollution from Ships |
| MBT | Motor blocks and turnings (types of scrap) |
| MDO | Marine diesel oil |
| MOLCHOPT | More or less in charterers' option (refers to cargo quantity) |
| MOLOO | More or less in owners' option |
| MV | Motor vessel |

**N**

| | |
|---|---|
| NAABSA | Not always afloat but safely aground |
| NCB | National Cargo Bureau |
| NDAS | No diesel at sea (refers to ship's fuel consumption) |
| NOPAC | North Pacific (US or Canada) |
| NOR | Notice of readiness |
| NRT | Net registered tonnage |
| NVOCC | Non vessel owning common carrier |
| NYPE | New York Produce Exchange (Charter Party for time charter trades) |

**O**

| | |
|---|---|
| OBL | Original bill of lading |
| OBO | Ore/bulk/oil carrying vessel |
| OBQ | Onboard quantity |
| OO | Owners' option |

**P**

| | |
|---|---|
| PC | Part cargo |
| PG | Persian Gulf (used when vessels are proceeding to Iranian ports) (see AG) |
| PMX | Panamax vessel |
| PMO | Passing Muscat outbound; i.e. exiting the Persian/Arabian Gulf |

**R**

| | |
|---|---|
| REDEL | Redelivery |
| RO/RO | Roll on roll off |
| ROB | Remaining on board (bunkers) |

**S**

| | |
|---|---|
| SA/SB/SP | Safe anchorage/safe berth/safe port |
| SBM | Single buoy mooring - used for loading tankers offshore OR Soybean meal |
| SBT | Segregated ballast tank |
| SCAC | Standard carrier alpha code – Four digit code used to identify transportation company |
| SF | Stowage factor |
| SHEX or SX | Sundays and holidays excluded |
| SHINC or SC | Sundays and holidays included |
| SMC | Safety management certificate |
| SOLAS | Safety of Life at Sea Convention |
| SOF | Statement of facts |
| SSO | Ship security officer |
| SSP | Ship security plan |
| SSW | Summer salt water |
| SWAD/SWDD | Salt water arrival draft/salt water departure draft |
| SWL | Safe working load (ship's gear) |

**T**

| | |
|---|---|
| TBN | To be named (or nominated) |
| TC - TCT | Time charter – time charter trip |
| TEU | Twenty foot container equivalent units |
| TIP | Taking inward pilot (contrast this to APS, arrival pilot station) |
| TPI | Tons per inch (immersion). Contrast TPC, tons per centimeter |
| TWIC | Transportation Worker's ID Card, allows bearer unescorted access in US ports |

**U**

| | |
|---|---|
| UBL | Unique bill of lading |
| ULCC | Ultra large crude (oil) carrier above 320,000 tons deadweight |
| UNCTAD | United Nations Conference on Trade and Development |
| UNLDD | Unleaded (gasoline) |
| USG | United States Gulf of Mexico |
| UU | Unless used |

**V**

| | |
|---|---|
| VLCC | Very large crude (oil) carrier above 160,000 tons deadweight |
| VLOO | Very large ore/oilers |

**W**

| | |
|---|---|
| W/M | Weight or measurement |
| WCCON | Whether customs cleared or not |
| WIBON | Whether in berth or not |
| WIFPON | Whether in free pratique or not |
| WLTHC | Waterline to top of hatch coaming |
| WOG | Without guarantee |
| WP | Weather permitting |
| WRI | War risks insurance |
| WVNS | Within vessel's natural segregations |
| WW | Weather working, or worldwide |
| WWD | Weather working day |

# Basics of Ship Charters

The following is a brief description of some of the basic elements of bareboat charters, time charters and voyage charters. This will provide a general overview of the responsibilities of the ship owner (or simply 'owner') and charterer. While many charter parties are drawn up on standardized forms (e.g. ASBATANKVOY or ASBATIME), the owner and charterer will usually add their own clauses and requirements to the charter agreement. Therefore, the particular charter party one deals with may differ from the basic terms discussed in this section.

**Charter or charter party** – a private contract or agreement by which a vessel (or in some cases, a part of a vessel) is made available (essentially leased) for use by someone other than the owner of the vessel.

## Owner/charterer

The *owner* is a person, company or corporation that legally owns the vessel (registered owner) or that contracts for the right to act as of the registered owner in order to charter the vessel to a third party (disponent owner).

The *charterer* is the person who contracts for the services of the ship. In some cases, the charterer may be the 'shipper' (exporter) or 'receiver' (importer) of a bulk commodity. In other cases, the charterer may even be another vessel owner who has contracted to transport cargo, but has no available ship of his own with which to move it.

## Types of charters

### Bareboat charter

In a bareboat charter, the charterer assumes complete control and operation of the vessel, for a specified period of time. The time period is usually lengthy, at the end of which the charterer must redeliver vessel in the same conditions as received, ordinary wear and tear excepted.

During the term of the charter, the charterer pays:

- Hire (paid monthly or semi-monthly in advance)
- crew
- fuel and boiler water
- provisions and stores
- repairs (except for latent defects)
- voyage expenses
- P&I insurance.

The owner pays:

- Hull and machinery insurance.

**Time charter**

In a time charter, the charterer gets full use of the vessel, but only partial control, for a specified period of time, during which he operates the vessel for his own account.

Terms and conditions can be adjusted to meet the needs of the parties involved, but standard terms allow for the following:

The owner pays:

- Financing (mortgages, etc.)
- hull, machinery and P&I insurance
- crew
- provisions and stores (including drinking water)
- repairs, including annual inspections (vessel goes off-hire), except repairs for damage caused by the charterer.

The charterer pays:

- Hire, calculated on a daily basis but paid monthly or semi-monthly in advance, unless otherwise negotiated
- fuel and boiler water
- voyage expenses (port fees, cargo expenses, etc.)
- repairs for damage caused by the charterer or its agents.

Off-hire is a term used for that period of time during which charter hire is not payable due to vessel or crew deficiencies, or for other reasons specified in the charter agreement. Off-hire does not apply to delays caused by the charterer, and the hire and fuel consumed during this period is usually deducted from the subsequent charter hire payment.

Under a time charter agreement, the Master may 'wear two hats,' meaning that he is employed by the owner, but may be an agent for the charterer when loading, discharging and trimming cargo.

**Voyage charter**

In a voyage charter, the charterer leases all or part of a vessel's cargo space for the purpose of transporting cargo between specific port. Under a voyage charter, there are no time limits set for the voyage, but the ship must arrive at the load port within a predetermined period (called the laydays/cancelling).

 **The owner retains control and full responsibility for operations of the vessel.**

The owner's obligations under a voyage charter are not limited to, but include:

- Delivery of the vessel to the charterer at a specified place or geographic range and within a specified time period
- financing
- insurance
- crew
- provisions and stores
- maintain the physical condition of the vessel
- fuel and boiler water
- voyage expenses.

Charterers are obliged to supply the specific cargo in the specific amount (within a tolerance, which can be 5%, 10% or might be minimum/maximum) at the specified port or range during a specific period. *This is an absolute obligation.*

**Consecutive voyage charter** is simply a contract for the performance of a number of successive voyages on one vessel, normally between the same loading and discharging ports. A consecutive voyage charter can also be for as many voyages as can be performed within a specific period of time.

**Contract of affreightment** (COA) usually covers an agreed amount of cargo to be moved between designated ports over a stipulated period of time by a fleet of vessels under one owner's control. It may be for a specific amount of cargo, or for all of a type of cargo that the shipper provides.

## Cargo expenses

The following different agreements for loading and discharging cargo may be negotiated:

- Liner terms or berth terms
    - the owner pays for all cargo handling costs including stevedoring
    - no guaranteed rate of loading and discharging by the charterer
    - no demurrage or despatch money
- Gross load terms
    - the owner pays for all cargo handling costs, including stevedoring
    - guaranteed rate of loading and discharging by the charterer
    - demurrage and despatch money
- FIO terms ('free in and out')
    - the charterer pays for all cargo handling costs including stevedoring

- the charterer guarantees loading and discharging rates
- demurrage and despatch money
- may be either 'free load' or 'free discharge' only. 'Free' means at no expense to the owner.

## Laytime, demurrage, dispatch money

- Laytime the number of days allowed for loading and discharging cargo.

- demurrage – the penalty paid by the charterer to the owner for exceeding the time allowed to load and/or discharge the cargo. A common shipping expression is *"Once on demurrage always on demurrage,"* meaning that, once the charterer exceeds the allowable laytime, demurrage will continue to accrue almost entirely without interruption.

- despatch money – paid to the charterer by the owner if the charterer completes loading or discharging before the laytime expire. Despatch money per day is usually one-half the demurrage per day.

## General average

The contributions and expenses that are incurred by the parties to a shipping venture (owners, charterers, cargo owners) after a serious incident occurs that may threaten both the vessel and its cargo. These contributions and expenses are deemed made for the common benefit and safety of all participants in the venture.

## Documents

The principal documents in marine transportation are (1) charter party agreements and (2) bills of lading (B/L). A B/L is a document of title, meaning that the holder of an original bill of lading has the right (provided they have paid the freight, if not prepaid) to demand from the ship owner the release of the cargo at the port of destination. A B/L is a separate contract between the shipper of the cargo and the holder of the B/L, and governs their respective rights and responsibilities.

## Laydays/canceling

The range of dates, anywhere between 3 and 15 days, is called laydays/canceling, or 'laycan'. This is the period of time specified in the charter party during which the owner must present his ship for use by the charterer at the place designated in the charter party. Unless the charter agreement provides otherwise, the first laycan date is the earliest date on which the charterer is required to accept notice of readiness after the ship has arrived at the first (or only) loading port. The last laycan date is the last day on which the charterer is obligated to accept notice of readiness for loading of cargo.

# Frequently used Shipping Terms

The terms in this glossary have been carefully selected from a myriad of terms one can encounter in the shipping business.

**Aboard**
Referring to cargo being put, or laden, onto a means of conveyance.

**About**
A term often used in maritime agreements to qualify cargo quantities, time periods, bunker quantities or a vessel's speed. For example, in the context of cargo quantities, 'about' usually implies a margin of plus or minus 5%.

**Air waybill**
The forwarding agreement or carrying agreement between shipper and air carrier and is issued only in non negotiable form.

**All in**
The total price to move cargo from origin to destination, inclusive of all charges.

**Alongside**
A phrase referring to the side of a ship. Goods delivered 'alongside' are to be placed on the dock or barge within reach of the transport ship's tackle so that they can be loaded.

**Astern**
- Behind a vessel
- move in a reverse direction.

**Bank guarantee**
Guarantee issued by a bank to a carrier to be used in lieu of lost or misplaced original negotiable bill of lading.

**Even keel**
Forward and aft draft are the same.

**Free pratique** – clearance by health authorities

**Hatch coaming**
Steel surrounding the hatch opening which rises vertically from the deck of the ship.

**Hatch cover**
Mechanism that covers hatch for weather protection.

**Inerting**
Reducing oxygen levels in gas tankers.

**Lien**
A legal claim upon goods for the satisfaction of some debt or duty.

**Load line - see marks**
Line at which the vessel has loaded maximum quantity of cargo.

**Longshoreman**
Individual employed in a port to load and unload ships.

**Manifest**
Document that lists in detail all the bills of lading issued by a carrier or its agent or master for a specific voyage. A detailed summary of the total cargo of a vessel. Used principally for customs purposes.

**Mate's receipt**
An acknowledgement of cargo receipt signed by a mate of the vessel. The possessor of the mate's receipt is entitled to the B/L, in exchange for that receipt.

**Meter**
39.37 inches (approximately) or 3.281 feet.

**Metric ton/m.t.**
2,204.6 pounds or 1,000 kilograms.

**Non-vessel operating common carrier (NVOCC)**
A cargo consolidator in ocean trades who will buy space from a carrier and sell it to smaller shippers.

**Ocean bill of lading (Ocean B/L)**
A contract for transportation between a shipper and a carrier. It also evidences receipt of the cargo by the carrier. A B/L shows ownership of the cargo and, if made negotiable, can be bought, sold or traded while the goods are in-transit.

**On board**
A notation on a B/L that cargo has been loaded on board a vessel. Used to satisfy the requirements of a letter of credit, in the absence of an express requirement to the contrary.

**Original bill of lading (OBL)**
A document which requires proper signatures for consummating carriage of contract. Must be marked as 'original' by the issuing carrier.

**Pier**
The structure perpendicular to the shoreline to which a vessel is secured for the purpose of loading and unloading cargo.

**Prepaid (PPD)**
Freight charges paid by the consignor (shipper) prior to the release of the bills of lading by the carrier.

**Quarantine**
A restraint placed on a vessel that has not been granted free pratique, due to a health hazard.

**Quay**
A structure attached to land to which a vessel is moored. See also pier and dock.

**Remittance**
Funds sent by one person to another as payment.

**Safe working load (SWL)**
Maximum safe lifting capacity of cargo handling gear.

**Sanction**
An embargo or restriction imposed by a government against another country.

**Ship's tackle**
All rigging, cranes, etc., utilized on a ship to load or unload cargo.

**Slop tank**
Tanks of vessel for storing residue that results from tank cleaning or hold cleaning.

**Starboard and port**
The right side (S) and left side (P) of a ship when facing the bow.

**Stern**
The rear of a vessel. Opposite of bow.

**Stevedore**
Individual or firm that employs longshoremen and who contracts to load or unload the ship.

**Tariff**
A publication setting forth the charges, rates and rules of transportation companies.

**Terminal charge**
A charge made for a service performed in a carrier's terminal area.

**Turnaround**
In water transportation, the time it takes between the arrival of a vessel and its departure.

**Weights and measures**

| Measurement ton | 40 cubic ft or one cubic meter. |
|---|---|
| Net ton, or short ton | 2,000 lbs. |
| Gross ton/long ton | 2,240 lbs. |
| Metric ton/kilo ton | 2,204.6 lbs. |
| Cubic meter | 35.314 cubic ft. |

**Wharfage**
Charge assessed by a pier or dock owner against freight handled over the pier or dock or against a steamship company using the pier or dock.

**Zulu time**
Time based on Greenwich Mean Time (GMT), so can also be referred to as UTC.

# Index

Accounting                                                        25, 95-96
After sailing service                                                 23-24
Agency and Agents, *see* Tramp Ship Agency and Tramp Ship Agent
Agency by necessity                                                      36
ASBA (Association of Ship Brokers and Agents (USA) Inc           78, 109

Baltic Exchange                                                          15
Bareboat (demise) charter                                          11, 123
Boarding agents                                         21, 22, 25, 109-112
Brokers, *see* Shipbroking
Bulk carriers                                                          8, 9

Cable broker                                                             16
Charter party agency clause                                           85-86
Charterer's agent provided competitive                                93-94
Charters
     Basics                                                       123-126
     Demise (bareboat) charter                                     11, 123
     Time charter                                                  12, 124
     Voyage charter                                        12-13, 124-125
Charterer
     Broker                                                          5, 16
     Liabilities                                                     85-89
     Market                                                             4
     Nominated agents                                         30-31, 65-67
     Responsibilities                                          12-13, 68-69
Classification societies                                                 10
Compensation                                                         58-59
Container ships                                                           8
Crude oil carriers                                                       9
Cruise ship agency fees                                                  94

Delivery and redelivery                                               72-73
Demise (bareboat) charter                                          11, 123
Demurrage                                                     13, 24, 126
Disbursements                          34, 52, 61-62, 70-72, 76-77, 93-96
Dry bulk carriers                                                        8

*Exxon Corp v Central Gulf Lines*                                        46

Freight market                                                        13, 17

Gas carriers                                                              9
General agent                                                        27-29

Hub agent                                                            32-24
Husbandry agent                                                  31-32, 69

Implied agency                                                      88-89
Insolvency                                                          76, 88
Institute of Chartered Shipbrokers                                     15
Insurance, protection and indemnity                               10, 61-63
*Interocean Shipping Company v National Shipping and Trading Corporation*      88

Law of agency                                                        35-39
   Agency by necessity                                    36
   Charterer's agent provided competitive              93-94
   Creation of                                         35-36
   Doctrine of implied agency                          88-89
   Implied authority                                       51
   Ratification                                       37, 89-90
   Signature                                          44-45, 52
   Termination                                          38-39
Laydays                                                              12, 53
Lien                                                        45-46, 59, 89, 127
Liner service                                                          2-3
Liquid bulk carriers (tankers)                                           9
Livestock carriers                                                       8
Lump sum agency fees                                                    93

*Minturn v Maynard*                                                     46
Multiport Shipping Agency                                               78

Nominated agents                                             30, 65-67, 85-91
Notice of readiness                                                     22
Notification of principal through agent                              54-55

Operations manager                                                 19-22, 25
Ore/bulk/oil carriers (OBOs)                                             9
Outsource agency services                                               34
Owner or time charterer's agent                                         30
Owner's broker                                                          16

P&I (Protection and Indemnity) clubs                           10, 61-62, 77
Port agency companies                                                18, 19
Port call                                                            21-23

| | |
|---|---:|
| Port costs request | 97-98 |
| Pre-arrival | 20-21 |
| Principals | 37 |
| Agency | 36-39 |
| Disclosed principal | 41-42 |
| Duties of agent to | 49-55 |
| Duties to agent | 57-59 |
| Maintenance of agent/principal relationship | 81-84 |
| Partly-disclosed principal | 42 |
| Relationship with agent and third parties | 41-43 |
| Undisclosed principal | 42 |
| Protecting or supervisory agent | 31 |
| | |
| Ratification | 37, 89-90 |
| Remedies of an agent | 59 |
| Ro/Ro vessels (roll on/roll off ships) | 8 |
| | |
| *Scrutton on Charter Parties* | 36 |
| Service fees | 92-93 |
| Ship's agent, *see* Tramp Ship Agent | |
| *Shipbrokers and the Law* (E.J. Edwards) | 49 |
| Shipbroking | 15-18 |
| Concepts and rules | 17 |
| Freight market | 17 |
| Types of shipbroker | 16 |
| Shipping industry | 1 |
| Signature | 43-44, 52 |
| Special agent | 29-30, 37 |
| | |
| Tanker broker | 16 |
| Tankers (liquid bulk carriers) | 9 |
| Tariff | |
| *Tarstar Shipping Company v Century Shipline Ltd* | 89 |
| Termination of agency | 38-39 |
| Third party rights against principal | 43 |
| Time charter | 12, 124 |
| Tramp Ship Agency | |
| Accounting | 95-96 |
| Communications | 96-99 |
| Creation of agency | 36 |
| Definition | 1 |
| Fees | 67, 91-94 |
| Law of agency | 35-39 |
| Marketing | 101-107 |
| Port agency companies | 18, 19 |
| Selection | 30, 57, 75-78, 81, 83, 85, 86, 89 |

| | |
|---|---|
| Ship agency networks | 78 |
| Staff | 25, 99-100 |
| Tramp agency services | 19-24 |
| Tramp Ship Agent | |
| Agent/Principal relationship | 1, 35-39, 41-42, 81-84, 102, 113-114 |
| "As agent" signature | 43-44, 52 |
| Authority | 41, 49 |
| Boarding agent | 21, 22, 25, 109-112 |
| Career | 109-112 |
| Charterer's nominated agent | 30 |
| Duties and liabilities of | 49-55 |
| Duties and liabilities to | 57-59 |
| Duties to Principal | |
| Contract signature | 52 |
| Confidentiality and loyalty | 50-51 |
| To account for funds | 52 |
| To act personally | 53 |
| To act within authority | 49-50 |
| To contract on Principal's behalf | 51 |
| To exercise care, skill and diligence | 52-53 |
| To keep Principal informed | 53 |
| Duty under time charter | 68-73 |
| General agent | 27-29 |
| Hub agent | 32-34 |
| Husbandry agent | 31-32, 69 |
| Insurance | 61-63 |
| Lien | 45-46 |
| Owner or time charterer's agent | 30 |
| Practical duties | 20-25, 54-55 |
| Protecting or supervisory agent | 31 |
| Remedies | 59 |
| Special agent | 29-30, 37 |
| Third party rights | 43 |
| Types of agent | 27-34 |
| Voyage charterer's nominated agent | 65-68 |
| Tramp Shipping | |
| Charters | 11-13 |
| Description | 7 |
| Operations and management | 9-11 |
| Owners and operators | 4-5, 7 |
| Types of vessel | 8-9 |
| Voyage charter | 12-13, 124-125 |
| Voyage charterer's nominated agent | 65-68 |
| Worldwide networks | 78 |